Design Patterns For Dummies®

Cheat Sheet

The 23 Gang of Four Design Patterns

Here are the original 23 Gang of Four design patterns (from *Design Patterns: Elements of Reusable Object-Oriented Software*, Addison-Wesley Professional Computing Series, by Erich Gamma, Richard Helm, Ralph Johnson, and John Vlissides).

The Strategy design pattern

Define a family of algorithms, encapsulate each one, and make them interchangeable. Strategy lets the algorithm vary independently from clients that use it.

The Decorator design pattern

Attach additional responsibilities to an object dynamically. Decorators provide a flexible alternative to subclassing for extending functionality.

The Factory Method design pattern

Define an interface for creating an object, but let subclasses decide which class to instantiate. Factory Method lets a class defer instantiation to subclasses.

The Observer design pattern

Define a one-to-many dependency between objects so that when one object changes state, all its dependents are notified and updated automatically.

The Chain of Responsibility design pattern

Avoid coupling the sender of a request to its receiver by giving more than one object a chance to handle the request. Chain the receiving objects and pass the request along the chain until an object handles it.

The Singleton design pattern

Ensure a class only has one instance, and provide a global point of access to it.

The Flyweight design pattern

Use sharing to support large numbers of fine-grained objects efficiently. A flyweight is a shared object that can be used in multiple contexts simultaneously. The flyweight acts as an independent object in each context — it's indistinguishable from an instance of the object that's not shared.

The Adapter design pattern

Convert the interface of a class into another interface clients expect. Adapter lets classes work together that couldn't otherwise because of incompatible interfaces.

The Facade design pattern

Provide a unified interface to a set of interfaces in a system. Facade defines a higher-level interface that makes the subsystem easier to use.

The Template design pattern

Define the skeleton of an algorithm in an operation, deferring some steps to subclasses. Template Method lets subclasses redefine certain steps of an algorithm without changing the algorithm's structure.

The Builder design pattern

Separate the construction of a complex object from its representation so that the same construction processes can create different representations.

Design Patterns For Dummies®

Cheat Sheet

The Iterator design pattern

Provide a way to access the elements of an aggregate object sequentially without exposing its underlying representation.

The Composite design pattern

Compose objects into tree structures to represent part-whole hierarchies. Composite lets clients treat individual objects and compositions of objects uniformly.

The Command design pattern

Encapsulate a request as an object, thereby letting you parameterize clients with different requests, queue or log requests, and support undoable operations.

The Mediator design pattern

Define an object that encapsulates how a set of objects interact. Mediator promotes loose coupling by keeping objects from referring to each other explicitly, and it lets you vary their interaction independently.

The State design pattern

Allow an object to alter its behavior when its internal state changes. The object will appear to change its class.

The Proxy design pattern

Provide a surrogate or placeholder for another object to control access to it.

The Abstract Factory design pattern

Provide an interface for creating families of related or dependent objects without specifying their concrete classes.

The Prototype design pattern

Specify the kinds of objects to create using a prototypical instance, and create new objects by copying this prototype.

The Bridge design pattern

Decouple an abstraction from its implementation so that the two can vary independently.

The Interpreter design pattern

Given a language, define a representation for its grammar along with an interpreter that uses the representation to interpret sentences in the language.

The Memento design pattern

Without violating encapsulation, capture and externalize an object's internal state so that the object can be restored to this state later.

The Visitor design pattern

Represent an operation to be performed on the elements of an object structure. Visitor lets you define a new operation without changing the classes of the elements on which it operates.

For Dummies: Bestselling Book Series for Beginners

Design Patterns

FOR

DUMMIES®

Design Patterns

FOR

DUMMIES®

by Steve Holzner, PhD

WILEY

Wiley Publishing, Inc.

Design Patterns For Dummies®

Published by
Wiley Publishing, Inc.
111 River Street
Hoboken, NJ 07030-5774

www.wiley.com

For general information on our other products and services, please contact our Customer Care Department within the U.S. at 800-762-2974, outside the U.S. at 317-572-3993, or fax 317-572-4002.

For technical support, please visit www.wiley.com/techsupport.

Wiley also publishes its books in a variety of electronic formats. Some content that appears in print may not be available in electronic books.

Library of Congress Control Number: 2006920631

ISBN-13: 978-0-471-79854-5

ISBN-10: 0-471-79854-1

Manufactured in the United States of America

10 9 8 7 6 5 4 3 2 1

1B/RX/QU/QW/IN

WILEY

About the Author

Steve Holzner is the award-winning author of 100 books on computing. He's a former contributing editor for *PC Magazine,* and has been on the faculty of Cornell University and MIT. In addition to his busy writing schedule, he gives programming classes to corporate programmers around the country and runs his own training company, which you can find at http://www.onsiteglobal.com/.

Dedication

To Nancy, as always and forever.

Author's Acknowledgments

The book you hold in your hands is the result of many peoples' work. I would particularly like to thank Mark Enochs, editor extraordinaire, and Katie Feltman, my acquisitions editor, who helped get this book off the ground and keep it in flight the rest of the way. Thanks also to my copy editor, Heidi Unger, for dotting the I's and crossing the T's.

Publisher's Acknowledgments

We're proud of this book; please send us your comments through our online registration form located at www.dummies.com/register/.

Some of the people who helped bring this book to market include the following:

Acquisitions, Editorial, and Media Development

Project Editor: Mark Enochs

Acquisitions Editor: Katie Feltman

Copy Editor: Heidi Unger

Technical Editor: John Purdum

Editorial Manager: Leah Cameron

Media Development Coordinator: Laura Atkinson

Media Project Supervisor: Laura Moss

Media Development Manager: Laura VanWinkle

Editorial Assistant: Amanda Foxworth

Cartoons: Rich Tennant (www.the5thwave.com)

Composition

Project Coordinator: Tera Knapp

Layout and Graphics: Carl Byers, Andrea Dahl, Lauren Goddard, Heather Ryan

Proofreaders: Debbye Butler, Christine Pingleton

Indexer: Techbooks

Publishing and Editorial for Technology Dummies

   Richard Swadley, Vice President and Executive Group Publisher

   Andy Cummings, Vice President and Publisher

   Mary Bednarek, Executive Acquisitions Director

   Mary C. Corder, Editorial Director

Publishing for Consumer Dummies

   Diane Graves Steele, Vice President and Publisher

   Joyce Pepple, Acquisitions Director

Composition Services

   Gerry Fahey, Vice President of Production Services

   Debbie Stailey, Director of Composition Services

Contents at a Glance

Table of Contents

Introduction

*I*f you're ever writing code and get the funny feeling that you've solved the problem you're working on before, you probably have. You may well have come across the same type of situation in the past, puzzled about it, and come up with the solution. And before that, you may have faced the same type of situation and come up with the same type of solution. And even before that . . . same thing.

Why keep reinventing the wheel? Why not just write down your solution and refer back to it as needed? That's what design patterns are all about. A design pattern represents a solution to a problem or class of problems that you can put to work at once in your own code.

In fact, design patterns go one step further — they also let you share in the solutions found by other programmers, and *expert* programmers at that. The design patterns you see in this book represent insightful solutions to dilemmas that just about every programmer comes up against sooner or later, and knowing them is going to save you a lot of time and effort.

Got a problem? Most likely, there's a design pattern for that. All you need to know is that someone has already solved your problem for you, with a careful eye towards good programming practices and efficiency. And all you have to do is apply that solution to your own code. Once you know how, there's nothing to it.

The design patterns covered in this book are essential for any programmer to know — and certainly for any professional programmer. There's a lot of ad hoc programming that goes on in the world, and that can lead to a lot of errors in critical code. Why be the one sitting in front of the debugger all day? Put design patterns to work for you and just slip the solution into place.

About This Book

There are plenty of design patterns floating around the programming world, and in time, a particular set of 23 of them has become accepted as the standard set. These patterns were first corralled in a book named *Design Patterns: Elements of Reusable Object-Oriented Software* (1995, Pearson Education, Inc. Publishing as Pearson Addison Wesley) by Erich Gamma, Richard Helm, Ralph Johnson, and John Vlissides — who have since been called the *Gang of Four*, or *GoF*, for short. And those 23 design patterns became known as the GoF design patterns.

You see all 23 of those standard patterns in this book, and some additional ones as well. I explain what each pattern does and when you should use the pattern. You also see a programming problem that the design pattern solves, implemented in code. In other words, every design pattern is put to work in easily understandable, runable code in this book.

In fact, some of the design patterns have already been put to work by the people who wrote the Java programming language. In such cases, I also discuss the part of Java that implements the design pattern already — such as closing windows in Swing or registering listeners with event-causing objects. Doing so gives you an immediate leg up with the design patterns covered — hey, you might find yourself saying: *That* looks familiar.

Foolish Assumptions

To fully understand how each pattern can make your life easier, you need to see it at work in a program, and this book uses the most widely used object-oriented programming language (Java) for its examples. For that reason, I assume you know Java.

You don't need to be a Java expert, though. If you can put together a program and work with objects, you'll be okay. You don't need to be a Java meister; the programming isn't super-challenging. The idea is to show each pattern at work with the easy-to-understand examples.

Besides Java, there's no special knowledge or skill needed to read this book. You don't have to know what patterns are or how they're put to work. All that's coming up in this book, from the most simple to the most powerful.

Conventions Used in This Book

Some books have a dozen dizzying conventions that you need to know before you can even start. Not this one. All you need to know is that new terms are shown in italics, like *this,* the first time they're discussed. And when new lines of code are introduced, they're displayed in bold, like this:

```
JButton button = new JButton("Check Spelling");
JTextField text = new JTextField(30);

public void init()
{
```

```
Container contentPane = getContentPane();

contentPane.setLayout(new FlowLayout());
    .
    .
    .
  button.addActionListener(new ActionListener()
  {
    public void actionPerformed(ActionEvent event) {
      text.setText("Good job.");
    }
  });
}
```

Note, also, that three vertical dots represent code that's been omitted. That's all there is to the notation in this book.

When I refer to something from the code, such as the name of an object or class, I set it off using a `monofont` typeface like this: Call the `draw` method.

How This Book Is Organized

Here are the various parts you see in this book:

Part 1: Getting to Know Patterns

Part I introduces patterns and how they make life easier. Chapter 1, "Congratulations, Your Problem Has Already Been Solved," shows how patterns fit into the scheme of things and how this book is going to make your programming problems easier to solve (no kidding). In the chapters that follow, you're introduced to the Strategy, Factory, Observer, and Singleton patterns, and more as you get to know patterns and how to work with them.

Part II: Becoming an OOP Master

Patterns rely heavily on object-oriented programming (OOP), and in this part, you see how patterns let you take charge of object-oriented work. I show you how to redefine steps of algorithms using subclasses with the Template Method pattern, how to convert an object's interface into a totally different interface with the Adapter pattern, how to handle object collections with the Iterator and Composite patterns, how to coordinate objects with the Command and Mediator patterns, and a great deal more in this part. After you read this part, you'll be an accomplished OOP meister.

Part III: The Part of Tens

Chapter 11 tells you about the remainder of the standard patterns, some of which are not in common use anymore, but all of which we cover in this book. Besides those standard patterns, you also see some newer patterns that have been added to the standard set of patterns, bringing us up to the modern day. Chapter 12 is all about joining the worldwide patterns community by creating your own pattern. You're going to see how to abstract a pattern from a set of problem solutions in this chapter and what it takes to introduce your new pattern to the world.

Icons Used in This Book

You find a couple of icons in this book, and here's what they mean:

This icon indicates something to remember, such as how you handle a particularly tricky part of a pattern.

This icon gives you something more — a behind-the-scenes way of working with a pattern, for example.

This icon means that what follows is technical, insider stuff. You don't have to read it if you don't want to, but if you want to become a pattern pro (and who doesn't?), take a look.

This icon tells you how not to fall into a pattern of trouble. Ignore this icon at your peril.

Where to Go from Here

Alright, you're all set and ready to jump into Chapter 1. You don't *have* to start there; you can jump in anywhere you like — the book is written to allow you to do just that. But if you want to get the full patterns story from the beginning, jump into Chapter 1 first — that's where all the action starts.

Also, for your convenience, all the code I provide in the book is available for downloading at www.dummies.com/go/designpatternsfd1e.

Part I
Getting to Know Patterns

In this part . . .

In this part, your guided tour of design patterns begins. Here, you see what patterns are all about. The idea is that other programmers have faced the same issues you're facing now and have come up with solutions that have been well tested. Through the use of patterns, they share their solutions with you, saving you lots of time and effort.

Chapter 1

Congratulations, Your Problem Has Already Been Solved

As a programmer, you know how easy it can be to get lost in the details of what you're doing. And when you lose the overview, you don't plan effectively, and you lose the bigger picture. When that happens, the code you're writing in the trenches ends up working fine for a while, but unless you understand the bigger picture, that code really is a specialized solution to a particular problem.

And the heck of it is that problems rarely stay solved after you've handled them once. Developers typically regard their work as tackling individual problems by writing code and solving those problems. But the truth is that in any professional environment, developers almost always end up spending a lot more time on maintenance and adapting code to new situations than writing entirely new code.

So if you consider it, it doesn't make sense to think in terms of Band-Aid fixes to remedy the problems you face because you'll end up spending a great deal of time putting out fires and trying to extend code written for a specific problem so that it can handle other cases as well. It makes more sense to get a little overview on the process of code design and maintenance.

The idea behind this book is to familiarize you with a set of *design patterns* to simplify the programming process automatically. The plan is to get you some overview automatically, no additional effort required. A design pattern is a tested solution to a standard programming problem. When you're familiar with the design patterns presented in this book, you can face a programming issue and — Bam! — a solution will come to you more quickly. Instead of banging your head against the wall in desperation, you'll say, "What I need here is the Factory pattern." Or the Observer pattern. Or the Adapter pattern.

That's *not* to say, as some design books seem to suggest, that you should spend a great deal of time dealing with abstractions and planning before tackling a project. Adding unneeded layers of abstraction to the programming process is not a burden any programmer needs.

The whole beauty here is simply that someone has already faced the problem you're facing and has come up with a solution that implements all kinds of good design. And being familiar with design patterns can make the design process all but automatic for you.

How do you turn into a software design expert, the envy of all, with hardly any work on your part? Easy. You read this book and get familiar with the patterns I cover in depth. You don't have to memorize anything; you just get to know those patterns. Then when you encounter a real-world issue that matches one of those patterns, something deep inside you says, "Hey! That looks like you need the Iterator pattern." And all you have to do is look up that pattern in this book and leaf through the examples to know what to do. So without further ado, this chapter gets you started on your tour of these handy, helpful design patterns.

Just Find the Pattern that Fits

The charm of knowing about design patterns is that it makes your solution easily reusable, extendable, and maintainable. When you're working on a programming problem, the tendency is to program to the problem, not in terms of reuse, extensibility, maintainability, or other good design issues. And that's where most programmers should be putting in more work because they end up spending far more time on such issues than on solving the original problem in the long run.

For example, you may want to create Java objects that can, say, parse XML documents. And to do that, you create a proprietary parser class, and then instantiate objects of that class to create XML parser objects as needed. So far, so good, you think. But it turns out that there are dozens of XML parser classes out there written in Java that people are attached to, and they might want to use the special features of the XML parser class they're used to. If you'd used the Factory pattern, you would have written code that could use any XML parser class to create parser objects (instead of hardcoding a proprietary solution). And your code would be extendable, reusable, and easier to maintain.

In other words, *design patterns are solutions to programming problems that automatically implement good design techniques.* Someone has already faced the issues you're facing, solved them, and is willing to show you what the best techniques are. All without a lot of memorization on your part; all you have to do is recognize which design pattern fits which situation and lock it into place.

Sweet.

Enter the Gang of Four Book

The set of 23 standard design patterns was published by Erich Gamma, Richard Helm, Ralph Johnson, and John Vlissides in their seminal 1995 book *Design Patterns: Elements of Reusable Object-Oriented Software* (Pearson Education, Inc. Publishing as Pearson Addison Wesley). They've come to be known in programming circles as the Gang of Four, or, more popularly, GoF.

A lot of water has passed under the bridge since the GoF book appeared, and it turns out that some of the original 23 patterns were not used as much as some of the others. You see them all in this book, but I emphasize the patterns that are used the most — and that includes some new, non-GoF patterns in Chapter 11 that have appeared since the GoF book debuted.

It's important to realize that there is more going on here than just memorizing design patterns. There are also specific design insights about object-oriented programming that are just as important, and I talk about them throughout the book. OOP is a terrific advance in programming. But too many programmers blindly apply its design strategies without a lot of insight, and that can cause as many problems as it fixes. A large part of understanding how to work with design patterns involves understanding the OOP insights behind them — encapsulating what changes most, for example, or knowing when to convert from is-a inheritance to has-a composites (see Chapter 2 for more on what these terms mean) — and I talk about those insights a lot.

Getting Started: The Mediator Pattern

Figure 1-1 provides an example design pattern, the Mediator pattern, that shows what design patterns can do for you. Say that you've got a four-page Web site that lets users browse a store and make purchases. As things stand, the user can move from page to page. But there's a problem — the code in each page has to know when to jump to a new page as well as how to activate the new page. You've got a lot of possible connections and a lot of duplicate code in the various pages.

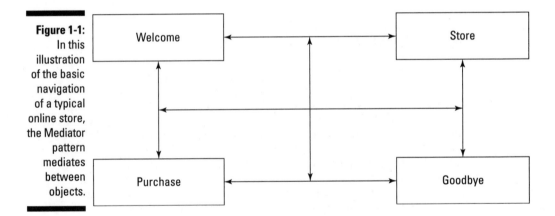

Figure 1-1: In this illustration of the basic navigation of a typical online store, the Mediator pattern mediates between objects.

You can use a mediator here to encapsulate all the navigation code out of the separate pages and place it into a mediator object instead. From then on, each page just has to report any change of state to the mediator, and the mediator knows what page to send the user to, as shown in Figure 1-2.

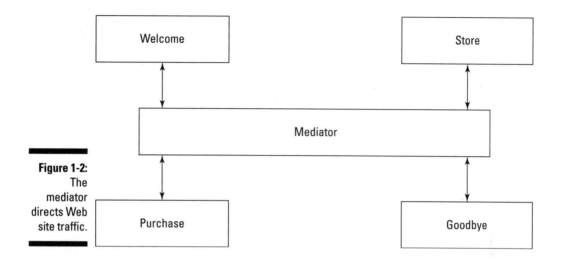

Figure 1-2:
The
mediator
directs Web
site traffic.

You can build the mediator to deal with the internals of each page so the various pages don't have to know the intimate details of the other pages (such as which methods to call). And when it's time to modify the navigation code that takes users from page to page, that code is all collected in one place, so it's easier to modify.

Adapting to the Adapter Pattern

Here's another design pattern, the Adapter pattern. Say that for a long time you've been supplied with a stream of objects and fit them into code that can handle those objects, as shown in Figure 1-3.

Figure 1-3:
Everything
seems to be
working
here.

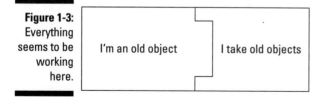

But now say there's been an upgrade. The code isn't expecting those old objects anymore, only new objects, and the old objects aren't going to fit into the new code, as shown in Figure 1-4.

Figure 1-4:
This isn't going to work.

I'm an old object

I only take new objects

If you can't change how the old objects are generated in this case, the Adapter pattern has a solution — create an adapter object that exposes the interface expected by the old object and the new code, and use the adapter to let the old object fit into the new code, as shown in Figure 1-5.

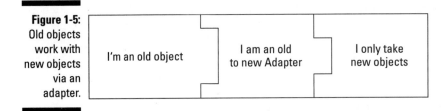

Figure 1-5:
Old objects work with new objects via an adapter.

I'm an old object

I am an old to new Adapter

I only take new objects

Problem solved. Who says design patterns are hard?

Standing In for Other Objects with the Proxy Pattern

Here's another pattern, the Proxy design pattern. Say that you've got some local code that's used to dealing with a local object as shown in Figure 1-6:

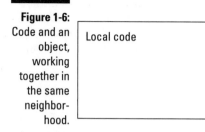

Figure 1-6:
Code and an object, working together in the same neighborhood.

Local code

Local object

But now say that you want to deal with some remote object, somewhere else in the world. How can you make the local code think it's dealing with a local object still when in fact it's working with that remote object?

With a *proxy.* A proxy is a stand-in for another object that makes the local code think it's dealing with a local object. Behind the scenes, the proxy connects to the remote object, all the while making the local code believe it's working with a local object, as you can see in Figure 1-7.

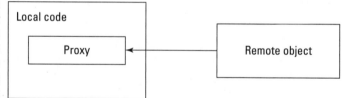

Figure 1-7:
Trick your local code and remote object into working together.

Local code

Proxy

Remote object

You see the Proxy pattern at work in Chapter 9 in an example that lets you connect to a remote object over the Internet anywhere in the world, with just a few lines of code.

Taking a Look at the Observer Pattern

You're most likely familiar with a number of the patterns in this book, such as the Observer pattern. This pattern, like many others, is already implemented in Java.

The Observer design pattern is about passing notifications around to update a set of objects when some important event has occurred. You can add new observer objects at runtime and remove them as needed. When an event occurs, all registered observers are notified. Figure 1-8 shows how it works; an observer can register itself with the subject.

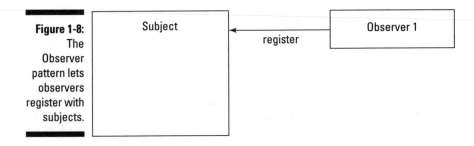

Figure 1-8: The Observer pattern lets observers register with subjects.

And another observer, Observer 2, can register itself as well, as shown in Figure 1-9.

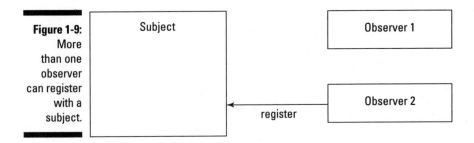

Figure 1-9: More than one observer can register with a subject.

Now the subject is keeping track of two observers. When an event occurs, the subject notifies both observers. (See Figure 1-10.)

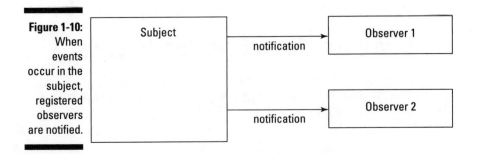

Figure 1-10: When events occur in the subject, registered observers are notified.

Does this sound familiar in Java? If Java event listeners came to mind, you'd be right. Event listeners can register with objects like push buttons or windows to be informed of any events that occur.

That's just one example of the kind of design pattern you've probably already seen implemented in Java. When such examples come up, I include Java example code showing how a particular design pattern is already built into Java. The example code might ring a few bells.

This book is written to be easy to use and understand. You're not going to see chalkboard diagrams of complex abstractions that you have to plow through. The chapters in this book are aimed at programmers, to be useful for programmers; even if you don't read all of them, you're going to benefit. The design insights and patterns covered here are becoming standard throughout the programming world, and they are helpful on an everyday level. Hopefully, the next time you face a tough coding issue, you'll suddenly find yourself saying: Aha! this is a job for the Facade pattern.

Chapter 2

Putting Plans into Action with the Strategy Pattern

As you, the design pattern expert, walk into the boardroom of MegaGigaCo, the CEO and members of the board are celebrating their new contract to design a set of cars in the sedate way you'd expect — by high-fiving each other and whooping around the room.

"This contract is going to mean a huge amount of income for us," says the CEO, sloshing a little champagne on the boardroom table in his excitement. "All we've got to do is make sure we get the design process right." He turns on the overhead projector, and as several large charts appear on the wall, the CEO says, "Now here's my idea . . ."

"Wrong," you say.

The CEO looks startled, and says, "But if we . . ."

"Nope," you say, shaking your head.

"What . . ."

"Sorry," you tell the CEO and the board, "it's clear you're risking your entire contract by doing things the wrong way. I can see a dozen problems just looking at that chart."

The board murmurs with concern and the CEO asks, "And you are?"

"I'm the design pattern pro who's going to solve all your design problems," you say. "For a whopping fee, of course."

The CEO writes down a tentative figure for your fee that, while large, doesn't seem large enough to you.

"Wrong again," you say.

The CEO looks at you with raised eyebrows.

"Design patterns," you explain, "represent solutions to known programming problems. Not only that, but they also represent good programming practice, making maintenance and extension of your code that much easier. So as you can see, hiring an expert like me makes a lot of sense — when I see a programming problem that has already been solved with a design pattern, I can tell you all about it."

"Well," the company programmers say reluctantly, "the idea behind design patterns sounds okay. But we already use object-oriented techniques in our programming. Doesn't that already cover the problem?"

"Nope," you say. In fact, that's one of the main points behind design patterns — they extend object-oriented programming (OOP).

Extending Object-Oriented Programming

Note the subtitle of the Gang of Four's *Design Patterns: Elements of Reusable Object-Oriented Software* (1995, Pearson Education, Inc. Publishing as Pearson Addison Wesley). Reuse is an important aspect of working with design patterns, and so is handling OOP issues. I discuss OOP first in this chapter, and then you'll see how working with OOP issues fits in with the Strategy pattern.

OOP was originally introduced as programs became larger and more complex. The idea was to wrap functionality inside objects. In other words, the inspiration was to divide and conquer. Until OOP appeared, you could divide your code into functions, but that wasn't enough in the long run. As programs became longer and longer, some way of dividing them up in terms of easily handled concepts was needed. What those concepts were, depended on the program itself, and those *concepts* came to be known as *objects*.

For example, if you take a look at what's going on in a kitchen behind the scenes, there's an enormous amount of complexity. A refrigerator can contain coolant pumps, thermostats, fans, lights, and more. A stove can contain various heating elements, timers, thermostats, lights, and more. Considered this way, looking at every present element at once, a kitchen becomes very complex.

But if you wrap what you see up into objects, the situation is a lot easier to handle. There's the refrigerator. There's the stove. That's the dishwasher, and so on. No problem — internal regulation and the various parts that work together are wrapped up into an easily conceptualized *object*.

That's why objects are called objects in object-oriented programming — you wrap functionality up into those objects and they're easily conceptualized, much like refrigerators, stoves, dishwashers, and so on. Exactly what those objects are, is up to you (which is why they're just generically called *objects,* and why you've never heard of refrigerator-oriented programming or stove-oriented programming).

For example, in a program, you may have an object named `display` that handles all the aspects of displaying your application's results. Another object might be named `database` to interact with a database server, and so forth. There can be a lot of complexity inside each object, but when you wrap everything up in a set of objects, life becomes a lot easier. You can work in terms of the `display` object and the few simple methods it exposes, not the `setRasterScanRate`, `populateVideoBuffer`, `adjustHorizontalHold` and dozens of other functions. That makes the programming a lot easier, which is why OOP became important as programs became longer and longer.

The big four OOP building blocks

There are four pillars of OOP — abstraction, encapsulation, polymorphism, and inheritance. I discuss these in the following sections.

Abstraction is the good kind of breakdown

A good part of working with design patterns involves *abstraction* — the careful consideration of how you're going to handle the problem. Abstraction isn't a programming technique; in essence, it just means that you conceptualize a problem before applying OOP techniques.

Abstraction is all about breaking your approach to a problem into natural segments. This is where you come up with the objects that divide the problem into manageable parts. In other words, abstracting a problem simply means thinking of how to tackle that problem in terms of object-oriented code. The data items needed by each object become that object's properties, whether public or private, and the actions each object needs to perform in the real world become its actions in code.

Much of what design patterns are all about has to do with making sure you're setting up the way you attack the problem correctly. Working with design patterns often means spending more time on the abstraction part of the process than on the concrete classes part.

Encapsulating all that junk

When you wrap methods and data up into an object, you *encapsulate* those methods and data. That's the power of working with objects — you remove the complexity from view and make it into an easily graspable object. That's how a mass of pipes, tubing, pumps, thermostats, and lights becomes, conceptually, a refrigerator.

When you encapsulate functionality into an object, you decide what interface that object exposes to the world. That refrigerator may handle a lot of complex actions behind the scenes, but you might want to put a dial in it to let the user tell the appliance how cold he wants his food. In the same way, you decide what getter and setter methods and/or public properties your objects present to the rest of the application so that the application can interact with it.

That's the idea behind encapsulation — you hide the complexities inside objects and then create a simple interface to let that object interact with the rest of your code. Design patterns are particularly big on encapsulation. One of the primary design insights here is that you should encapsulate what changes the most. A number of patterns revolve around that idea — extracting the part of your code that changes the most, or that needs the most maintenance, and encapsulating that part into its own object for easier handling. You see a lot about encapsulation and how to put it to work in unexpected ways to solve common problems in this book.

Mighty polymorphism rangers

Another cornerstone of OOP is *polymorphism:* the ability to write code that can work with different object types and decide on the actual object type at runtime. For example, you might want to write code that handles all kinds of different shapes — rectangles, circles, triangles, and so on. Although they're different shapes, they all have in common certain actions as far as your code goes — for example, they can all be drawn.

Using polymorphism, you can write your code to perform various actions on the shapes you're working with — and then decide on the actual shape(s) you want to use at runtime. *Polymorphic* (which means *many form*) code works with any such shape without being rewritten.

Start with this Shape class that draws a generic shape when you call its draw method:

```
class Shape
{
  public void draw()
  {
    System.out.println("Drawing a shape.");
  }
}
```

Then you extend a new class, Rectangle, from Shape, and let it draw a rectangle when you call its draw method as follows:

```
class Rectangle extends Shape
{
  public void draw()
  {
    System.out.println("Drawing a rectangle.");
  }
}
```

Want to draw a shape? No problem. You just write some code to create an object named shape and call the object's draw method:

```
public class Polymorphism
{

  public static void main(String[] args)
  {
    Shape shape = new Shape();

    shape.draw();
  }
}
```

Running this example gives you this:

```
Drawing a shape.
```

Want to draw a rectangle using the same code? No problem. Through the magic of polymorphism, just reload the shape variable with a rectangle object instead and then proceed with the same code as before:

```
public class Polymorphism
{

  public static void main(String[] args)
  {
    Shape shape = new Shape();
    shape = new Rectangle();

    shape.draw();
  }
}
```

Running this code gives you:

```
Drawing a rectangle.
```

In the first case, you loaded a shape object into the shape variable and then called its draw method. In the second case, you took a rectangle object and loaded it into that same variable, shape — even though that variable was declared to be a shape object — and then called the draw method again to draw a rectangle.

So you used the same variable, shape, to hold a shape object and a rectangle object, which works because rectangle is derived from shape. In this way, you can decide what type of object to load into the shape variable at runtime, leaving your code unchanged.

Inheritance without the pesky taxes

The last of the formal cornerstones of OOP is *inheritance:* the process by which one class can inherit methods and properties from another. You just saw inheritance at work (in the previous section) — starting with the Shape class as shown here:

```
class Shape
{
  public void draw()
  {
    System.out.println("Drawing a shape.");
  }
}
```

Then deriving the `Rectangle` class from `Shape`, as you see here:

```
class Rectangle extends Shape
{
  public void draw()
  {
    System.out.println("Drawing a rectangle.");
  }
}
```

Polymorphism often comes into play when you work with design patterns because design patterns tend to favor *composition* over inheritance. (You use composition when your object contains other objects instead of inheriting from them.) Inheritance sets up "is-a" relationships — Rectangle "is-a" Shape, for example. As you're going to see, however, that can introduce unexpected rigidity and problems into your code, especially when it comes time to maintain that code.

Design pattern-oriented programming often prefers object composition over inheritance. When you use composition, your code contains other objects, rather than inheriting from them. And to be supple enough to deal with the various kinds of contained objects in the same way, with the same code, design-patterns often rely on polymorphism.

Composition versus inheritance: A first attempt at designing the new cars

So who says that you should favor composition over inheritance? Perhaps an example will help. The programmers at MegaGigaCo (from the beginning of the chapter) know all about inheritance, and they've started designing the new cars despite your warnings to wait until you've had the chance to talk with them. They know they're supposed to be designing a series of vehicles, so they've started by creating a base class named `Vehicle` with a method named `go` that displays the text `Now I'm driving`.

```
public abstract class Vehicle
{
  public Vehicle()
  {
  }

  public void go()
  {
    System.out.println("Now I'm driving.");
  }
}
```

Then they've created new classes, such as `StreetRacer`, using `Vehicle` as a base class like so:

```
public class StreetRacer extends Vehicle
{
  public StreetRacer()
  {
  }
}
```

So far, so good. If you create a new `StreetRacer` and run it like this:

```
public static void main(String[] args)
{
  StreetRacer streetRacer = new StreetRacer();

  streetRacer.go();
        .
        .
        .
}
```

Then you're going to see:

```
Now I'm driving.
```

That looks fine. So fine, in fact, that MegaGigaCo decides to run with it and comes out with a Formula One racer that also extends the `Vehicle` class as you can see in the following:

```
public class FormulaOne extends Vehicle
{
  public FormulaOne()
  {
  }
}
```

And you can run both the street racer and the Formula One racer this way:

```
public static void main(String[] args)
{
  StreetRacer streetRacer = new StreetRacer();
  FormulaOne formulaOne = new FormulaOne();

  streetRacer.go();
  formulaOne.go();
        .
        .
        .
}
```

And you get:

```
Now I'm driving.
Now I'm driving.
```

Not bad, say the CEO and the board. Who needs design patterns? they ask, shooting you dirty looks. But then they get a contract to produce *helicopters*. Helicopters, they reason, are just another type of vehicle. So they create helicopters using a Helicopter class, extending the Vehicle class like this:

```
public class Helicopter extends Vehicle
{
  public Helicopter()
  {
  }
}
```

But now there's a problem — if you run the helicopter in addition to the cars like this:

```
public static void main(String[] args)
{
  StreetRacer streetRacer = new StreetRacer();
  FormulaOne formulaOne = new FormulaOne();
  Helicopter helicopter = new Helicopter();

  streetRacer.go();
  formulaOne.go();
  helicopter.go();
       .
       .
       .
}
```

Then you get this when you run all three vehicles: one street racer, one Formula One race car, and one helicopter:

```
Now I'm driving.
Now I'm driving.
Now I'm driving.
```

That doesn't look right, says the CEO doubtfully. Why should the helicopter be driving? Shouldn't it be flying? And the problem only gets worse when MegaGigaCo gets a contract to produce jets, which they also extend from the Vehicle class:

```
public class Jet extends Vehicle
{
  public Jet()
  {
  }
}
```

Running all four vehicles — street racer, Formula One race car, helicopter, and jet, now gives you this:

```
Now I'm driving.
Now I'm driving.
Now I'm driving.
Now I'm driving.
```

That's definitely not right, says the CEO. Jets don't drive when they're in the air. They fly — and fast. No problem, say the company programmers. We can just override the `go` method in the `Helicopter` and `Jet` classes to give the right behavior. They create something like this, which makes the `Helicopter` class fly, not drive:

```
public class Helicopter extends Vehicle
{
  public Helicopter()
  {
  }

  public void go()
  {
    System.out.println("Now I'm flying.");
  }
}
```

"Okay," says the CEO, "but the board of directors has already voted to change that from 'Now I'm flying.' to 'Now I'm flying at 200 mph' next week. And more changes will be coming later, if I know them."

There's a problem here, you explain, and it's that the company programmers are spreading the way a single task is accomplished — driving a car or flying a helicopter — across several generations of classes. That's not necessarily a big problem, but if how you want to handle that task is going to change fairly often, as here, having to edit all those classes becomes a maintenance issue.

You say: maybe inheritance isn't the answer in a case like this, where you have to *spread out the handling of a changeable task over several generations of classes*. You're going to be maintaining a lot of customized code across generations of classes when that task changes. And as the derived classes get to be long and involved, it's going to be tough to maintain them through all those changes. You're going to have to update the `go` method forever.

The problem you're trying to solve is how to avoid spreading out the handling of a particular, changeable task over several generations of classes. If you don't avoid that, you'll be editing a lot of files to update your code.

Perhaps there's a better way of handling the task of making vehicles move than using inheritance in this case. Hey, says a company programmer — how about using interfaces instead of using inheritance? You could set up an IFly interface and give that interface a method named go that the Helicopter class has to implement as shown in the following:

```
public class Helicopter implements IFly
{
  public Helicopter()
  {
  }

  public void go()
  {
    System.out.println("Now I'm flying.");
  }
}
```

No good, you say. You haven't solved the problem at all — each class and subclass still has to implement its own version of the go method, which is just as bad as when you used inheritance. And because interfaces don't include code, you still have to write custom code in each class, which means code reuse goes out the window.

Handling Change with "has-a" Instead of "is-a"

Things change. In commercial development, things change a lot, so it's worthwhile planning for it. If you've got a small problem that needs a small solution, you probably won't have to plan for a great deal of change. But if you're working on a serious project of some substantial size and it's going to be around for a while, you should start thinking in terms of change. The requirements your code must meet will vary over time, and you will have to modify your code at some point in the future to handle those evolving requirements. Most developers don't take this potential for change into account, and they invariably regret it later. How big does a project have to be before you should code to allow for graceful change? That's a judgment call, part of the art of programming. By understanding how to handle change, you'll know better when to allow for it.

Here's a design insight that you may have seen mentioned: Separate the parts of your code that will change the most from the rest of your application and try to make them as freestanding as possible for easy maintenance. You should also always try to reuse those parts as much as possible.

What this means is that if part of your application changes a lot, get it out of those large files that otherwise change very little and make the sections that change a lot as freestanding as you can so that you can make changes as easily as possible while reducing side effects. And if you can, reuse the separated components that change a lot so that if you need to make a change, that change will be made automatically throughout the many places in the code that use those components.

Here's how to think about this way of planning for change, and why inheritance often can't handle change very well. With inheritance, base classes and derived classes have an "is-a" relationship. That is, a Helicopter "is-a" Vehicle, which means Helicopter inherits from Vehicle, and if you have to customize the methods you inherit a great deal, you're going to run up against maintenance issues in the future. The base class handles a particular task one way, but then a derived class changes that, and the next derived class down the line changes things yet again. So you've spread out how you handle a task over several generations of classes.

If, on the other hand, you can extract the volatile parts of your code and encapsulate them as objects, you can use those objects as you need them — and the entire task is handled by the code in such an object, it's not spread out over generations of classes. Doing so allows you to customize your code by creating composites of objects. With composites, you select and use the objects you want, instead of having a rigid hard-coded internal way of doing things. That gives you a "has-a" relationship with those objects — a street racer "has-a" certain way of moving, which is encapsulated in an object; a helicopter "has-a" different way of moving, which is also encapsulated in an object. And each object performs a task.

One object, one task often makes sense instead of writing multi-generation code where one task is spread out over a dozen generations. In other words, you're reorganizing around the *tasks,* not around the generations of classes that inheritance gives you.

Using inheritance automatically sets things up in terms of strict, inclusive "is-a" relationships, which is more likely to cause maintenance and extensibility issues down the line. If you want to plan for change, it usually helps to think as much as you can in terms of "has-a" relationships, where your code has a number of objects whose code can be more easily updated as change happens.

When planning for change, consider "has-a" instead of "is-a" relationships, and put volatile code in the objects your application contains, rather than inheriting that code.

Drawing Up Your Plans

How would the idea of separating out volatile code work in the Vehicle/ StreetRacer/Helicopter example in this chapter? According to the CEO, the part that is going to be changing the most is the go method, so that's the part to separate out. In design pattern terms, each implementation of the go method is called an *algorithm* (basically that's just another name for a strategy). So you want to create a set of algorithms that can be used by your various StreetRacer, FormulaOne, Helicopter, and Jet objects. Doing so separates the volatile code into algorithms. Each algorithm handles one complete task, so you don't have to spread out the handling of that task over generations of classes.

Creating your algorithms

To make sure that all the algorithms implement the same methods (that's just the go method here), you need to create an interface, the GoAlgorithm interface, which all algorithms must implement:

```
public interface GoAlgorithm
{
  public void go();
}
```

The GoAlgorithm interface has one method: go. To make sure any algorithm can be used by any Vehicle, all algorithms should implement this interface, which means they all have to define a go method. The first algorithm, GoByDrivingAlgorithm, displays Now I'm driving. Here's what the GoByDrivingAlgorithm looks like:

```
public class GoByDrivingAlgorithm implements GoAlgorithm
{
  public void go()
  {
    System.out.println("Now I'm driving.");
  }
}
```

The GoByFlying algorithm, on the other hand, displays Now I'm flying.

```
public class GoByFlying implements GoAlgorithm
{
  public void go() {
    System.out.println("Now I'm flying.");
  }
}
```

And the `GoByFlyingFast` algorithm, used by jets, displays `Now I'm flying fast.`

```
public class GoByFlyingFast implements GoAlgorithm
{
  public void go()
  {
    System.out.println("Now I'm flying fast.");
  }
}
```

Great. You just separated algorithms from your code. You're starting to implement "has-a" rather than "is-a" design techniques. Now you've got to put those algorithms to work.

Using your algorithms

Now you've got a number of algorithms you can create objects from in order to build your code using "has-a", not "is-a", relationships. After you create an object from an algorithm, you've got to store that object somewhere, so I'll add a new method to the `Vehicle` base class, `setGoAlgorithm`. That method stores the algorithm you want to use in an internal, private variable, `goAlgorithm` as shown in the following:

```
public abstract class Vehicle
{
  private GoAlgorithm goAlgorithm;

  public Vehicle()
  {
  }

  public void setGoAlgorithm (GoAlgorithm algorithm)
  {
    goAlgorithm = algorithm;
  }
    .
    .
    .
}
```

Now when you want to use a particular algorithm in a derived class, all you've got to do is to call the `setGoAlgorithm` method with the correct algorithm object, this way:

```
setGoAlgorithm(new GoByDrivingAlgorithm());
```

The `Vehicle` class's `go` method also has to change. Previously, it just displayed the message `Now I'm driving`.

```
public void go()
{
  System.out.println("Now I'm driving.");
}
```

Now, however, it has to call the `go` method defined in the algorithm, so here's how the new code works:

```
public abstract class Vehicle
{
  private GoAlgorithm goAlgorithm;

  public Vehicle()
  {
  }

  public void setGoAlgorithm (GoAlgorithm algorithm)
  {
    goAlgorithm = algorithm;
  }

  public void go() {
    goAlgorithm.go();
  }
}
```

Now all you have to do is select which algorithm you want to use for which vehicle. For example, the street racer will use `GoByDrivingAlgorithm`:

```
public class StreetRacer extends Vehicle
{
  public StreetRacer()
  {
    setGoAlgorithm(new GoByDrivingAlgorithm());
  }
}
```

The Formula One race car will also use `GoByDrivingAlgorithm`:

```
public class FormulaOne extends Vehicle
{
  public FormulaOne()
  {
    setGoAlgorithm(new GoByDrivingAlgorithm());
  }
}
```

But the helicopter will use `GoByFlyingAlgorithm`:

```
public class Helicopter extends Vehicle
{
  public Helicopter()
  {
    setGoAlgorithm(new GoByFlyingAlgorithm());
  }
}
```

And the jet will use `GoByFlyingFastAlgorithm`:

```
public class Jet extends Vehicle
{
  public Jet()
  {
    setGoAlgorithm(new GoByFlyingFastAlgorithm());
  }
}
```

It's time to put this to the test. Just compile and run `StartTheRace.java`, as well as the needed `Helicopter.java`, `Jet.java`, and other files in the downloadable code for this book. `StartTheRace.java` creates an object of each vehicle type and calls each `go` method:

```
public class StartTheRace
{

  public static void main(String[] args)
  {
    StreetRacer streetRacer = new StreetRacer();
    FormulaOne formulaOne = new FormulaOne();
    Helicopter helicopter = new Helicopter();
    Jet jet = new Jet();

    streetRacer.go();
    formulaOne.go();
    helicopter.go();
    jet.go();

  }
}
```

And here's what you get:

```
Now I'm driving.
Now I'm driving.
Now I'm flying.
Now I'm flying fast.
```

Just what you wanted, except now you're using "has-a" relationships instead of inheritance-based "is-a" relationships. All kinds of code can use these algorithms because the code in these algorithms is no longer buried in the `StreetRacer`, `Helicopter`, and other classes.

This technique gives you an alternative to subclassing and inheritance. If you use "is-a" inheritance, you may end up spreading out how you handle a particular task in the base class and all derived classes — as when you overrode the `go` method for helicopters and jets. If you use the "has-a" model, you can create a well-defined family of algorithms — as many as you need — and then choose the algorithm you want to use.

In this way, you're been able to overcome a problem that inheritance causes for many programmers: If you have to spread out how you handle a task across several generations of classes, and how you handle that task changes a lot, you're going to be editing a lot of code as you maintain it. If, on the other hand, you can concentrate how you handle that task into a single algorithm object, changes will be a lot easier to handle.

The board of directors says the message should change from `Now I'm flying.` to `Now I'm flying at 200 mph.` No problem, just change that in the `GoByFlying` algorithm:

```java
public class GoByFlying implements GoAlgorithm
{
  public void go() {
    System.out.println("Now I'm flying at 200 mph.");
  }
}
```

Now all the code that uses this algorithm is updated automatically; no need to go searching through a lot of class files. In this way, when you concentrate how you handle a task into a single algorithm object, you have a lot more control over that task, especially when you want to make changes to it.

Selecting algorithms at runtime

"Wait a minute," the CEO of MegaGigaCo says. "It occurs to me that jets don't just 'fly fast.' They drive for a while along the runway first. And when they land, they drive along the runway too. So shouldn't their behavior be drive, fly fast, and then drive again?"

"Theoretically, yes," groan the company programmers. "But that would take a lot of extra code."

"Not at all," you say. "That's one of the charms of using external algorithm objects — you can change the behavior you want at runtime."

When you hardcode a task into your class files, you can't switch tasks at runtime. But when you use external algorithm objects in a "has-a" relationship, it's easy to switch at runtime. In other words, the "has-a" relationship can give you more flexibility than the "is-a" relationship when it comes to configuring behavior at runtime.

Here's how selecting algorithms dynamically works in a new example, RealJet.java. To make the jet taxi, you create a new Jet object and set the jet's algorithm to the GoByDrivingAlgorithm, as shown in the following code:

```
public class RealJet
{

  public static void main(String[] args)
  {
    Jet jet = new Jet();

    jet.setGoAlgorithm(new GoByDrivingAlgorithm());
       .
       .
       .

}
```

To make the jet drive along the runway, use its go method:

```
public class RealJet
{

  public static void main(String[] args)
  {
    Jet jet = new Jet();

    jet.setGoAlgorithm(new GoByDrivingAlgorithm());
    jet.go();
       .
       .
       .

}
```

You can call the jet's setGoAlgorithm to change the jet's go algorithm dynamically, then call the go method again after each time you change that algorithm:

```
public class RealJet
{

  public static void main(String[] args)
  {
    Jet jet = new Jet();

    jet.setGoAlgorithm(new GoByDrivingAlgorithm());
    jet.go();

    jet.setGoAlgorithm(new GoByFlyingFastAlgorithm());
    jet.go();

    jet.setGoAlgorithm(new GoByDrivingAlgorithm());
    jet.go();
  }
}
```

Here are the results — the jet taxis, flies, and then taxis again, no problem:

```
Now I'm driving.
Now I'm flying fast.
Now I'm driving.
```

As you see, switching algorithms at runtime is no problem. On the other hand, if you had hardcoded specific behavior into the jet, there would have been no way to change it at runtime. In other words, you can set the strategy you want to use at runtime. All of which brings us to the design pattern for this chapter, which this chapter's whole discussion has really been about — the Strategy design pattern.

Making Your Move with the Strategy Pattern

The Strategy design pattern is the first one covered in this book, and in fact you've seen it at work throughout this chapter already. This design principle comes into play when it makes sense to extract code that handles specific tasks from your app.

Creating a family of algorithms lets you choose your strategy by choosing consciously which algorithm(s) you want to work with. This design pattern is often used as an alternative to inheritance, where you can end up spreading out the way you handle one specific task over many class files.

Here's the problem, in general. You may find yourself implementing a single task across several generations of classes. At first, everything is fine, you handle the task in one class alone, as shown in Figure 2-1.

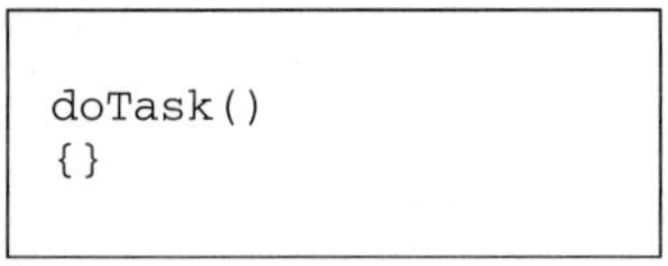

Figure 2-1:
One object,
one task.

```
doTask()
{}
```

But as time goes on, special cases seem to require new classes, and you use inheritance and overriding code in the inheriting classes, spreading the way you handle the single task across a number of inheriting classes (see Figure 2-2).

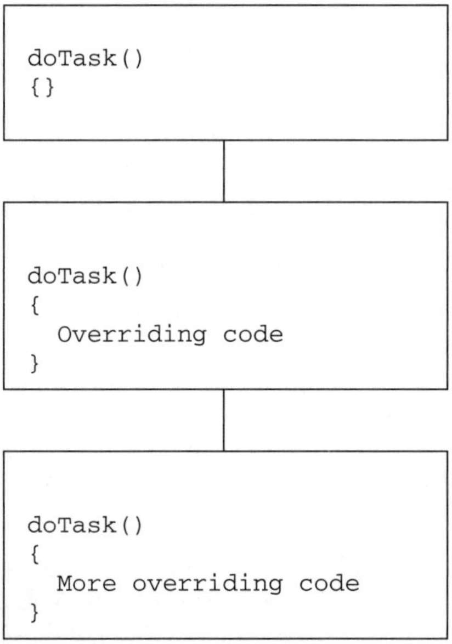

```
doTask()
{}
```

```
doTask()
{
    Overriding code
}
```

Figure 2-2:
Adding
tasks
requires
rewriting
code.

```
doTask()
{
    More overriding code
}
```

The Strategy design pattern says that you should extract the volatile parts of your code and encapsulate them as objects; you can use those objects as you need them. Now you can customize your code by creating composites of objects. At runtime, you just use polymorphism to choose the object(s) you want to work with, as shown in Figure 2-3.

Figure 2-3:
The
Strategy
pattern
saves you
time in the
long run.

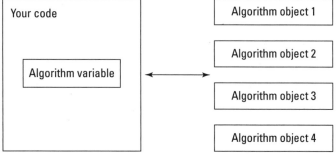

Your code	Algorithm object 1
Algorithm variable ←——→	Algorithm object 2
	Algorithm object 3
	Algorithm object 4

The GoF book says the Strategy design pattern should: "Define a family of algorithms, encapsulate each one, and make them interchangeable. Strategy lets the algorithm vary independently from clients that use it."

The Strategy design pattern points out that, sometimes, it's good to be task-oriented. That's especially important if you want to maintain volatile code away from the main code for your app, or if you want to change the algorithm you use at runtime.

Consider using the Strategy design pattern if you have one of the following situations:

- ✔ You have volatile code that you can separate out of your application for easy maintenance.
- ✔ You want to avoid muddling how you handle a task by having to split implementation code over several inherited classes.
- ✔ You want to change the algorithm you use for a task at runtime.

So there you have it — any time you start to get task-oriented and want to make those tasks one of the main design points of your code, the Strategy design pattern should spring to mind. That's the way design patterns work. They don't provide you with specific code. Instead, you familiarize yourself with the idea, and when that idea could come in handy there's an Aha! moment. This looks like a job for the Strategy pattern!

Knowing how various design patterns work also gives you a way of talking to other people who are familiar with those design patterns. Most professional programmers should know at least some standard design patterns. When someone on your team starts talking about using the Strategy design pattern and everyone starts nodding knowingly, you want to be able to nod knowingly as well.

Chapter 3

Creating and Extending Objects with the Decorator and Factory Patterns

· ·

In This Chapter

▶ Keeping code closed for modification, open for extension

▶ Introducing the Decorator pattern

▶ Creating your own decorators

▶ Wrapping objects in decorators

▶ Building objects with factories

▶ Encapsulating object creation in factories

▶ Using the Factory Method pattern

· ·

You're on the job as the new Design Pattern consultant at GigantoComputer company, getting paid an exorbitant amount of money, and you're in the company cafeteria.

"What'll you have?" asks the surly cook behind the grill counter.

"A burger," you say, wrestling with your tray.

The cook rings it up on the cash register, and then remembers to ask, "Fries with that?"

"Sure," you say.

The cook clears the order on the cash register and starts over, saying, "Burger and fries," and enters that.

"Let's make that a cheeseburger," you say on impulse.

The cook gives you a dirty look and starts the order over from scratch, pecking at the keyboard and saying, "Burger with cheese and fries. Okay. That it?"

"Hmm," you say, scanning the posted menu. "Maybe make that a bacon cheeseburger."

The cook stares at you and seems on the verge of saying something unpleasant, but enters the order into the cash register, starting the whole process over.

"Hey," you say, "you sure could benefit by using the Decorator design pattern, eh?"

"Yeah," says the cook, wondering what you're talking about. "I've said the same thing a thousand times."

You take your bacon cheeseburger with fries happily, and ask, "How about some tomato slices on that?"

This chapter is all about two important design patterns that take care of flaws in standard object-oriented programming, especially when it comes to inheritance: the Decorator and Factory patterns.

The Decorator pattern is perfect for the opening scenario I just outlined because it's all about extending the functionality of a given class. After you've written a class, you can add decorators (additional classes) to extend that class; doing so means that you won't have to keep modifying the original class's code over and over again. So your burger can become a cheeseburger, and then a bacon cheeseburger, with no extra trouble.

As I discuss later in the chapter the Factory design pattern is a well-known and popular one, which does something a little different. Using this design pattern lets you improve the Java new operator by giving you a lot more flexibility when you create new objects. When you use this pattern, you use your own code to create new objects; you don't use just the new operator. There's an interesting twist here, though: what a lot of programmers think of as the Factory design pattern is not the actual Gang of Four (GoF) Factory design pattern. I look at both the popular and formal versions of the Factory design pattern in this chapter.

Note: For more on OOP, you might take a look at *Java All-In-One Desk Reference For Dummies,* by Doug Lowe, Wiley Publishing, Inc. But we're not going to tackle more OOP than you have already encountered as a Java programmer in any case.

Closed for Modification, Open for Extension

One of the most important aspects of the development process that developers and programmers have to grapple with is *change,* which is why design patterns were introduced in the first place. In particular, design patterns are intended to help you handle change as you have to adapt your code to new and unforeseen circumstances. As I mention throughout this book, developers spend much more time extending and changing code than they do originally developing it.

The Strategy design pattern introduced in Chapter 2 is all about helping you handle change by letting you select from a family of external algorithms rather than having to rewrite your code. The Decorator pattern is similar, in that it allows you to write your code and avoid modification, while still extending that code if needed. That's one of the major design points that I want to emphasize.

As much as possible, make your code closed for modification, but open for extension. In other words, design your core code so that it doesn't have to be modified a lot, but may be extended as needed.

Here's an example that makes keeping your core code closed for modification more clear. Say that the company you're working for as a consultant, GigantoComputer, decides to make a new computer. Here's the code for the Computer class:

```
public class Computer
{
  public Computer()
  {
  }

  public String description()
  {
    return "You're getting a computer.";
  }
}
```

When a new computer object is created, its description method returns the text You're getting a computer. So far, so good. But some customers decide that they want a hard disk in their computers. "No problem," the company programmers say. "We can just change the code this way":

```
public class Computer
{
  public Computer()
  {
  }

  public String description()
  {
    return "You're getting a computer and a disk.";
  }
}
```

Now when a new `computer` object is created and you call its `description` method, you get the text `You're getting a computer and a disk`. But some customers are never satisfied — they want a monitor too. So the company programmers change the code again to this:

```
public class Computer
{
  public Computer()
  {
  }

  public String description()
  {
    return "You're getting a computer and a disk and a monitor.";
  }
}
```

Now when you create a `computer` object and call its `description` method, you'll see:

```
You're getting a computer and a disk and a monitor.
```

You can see the issue here: The company programmers have to change the code every time someone wants to customize his or her computer purchase. Obviously, that's a problem.

And you, the high-power design patterns consultant, can fix it.

Enter the Decorator Pattern

I can't say this enough, and to prove it, I'm going to say it again: As much as possible, make your code closed for modification but open for extension. In Chapter 2, you get an idea how that works with the Strategy design pattern. There, you encapsulate code in external algorithms for easy use rather than spreading it around inside your core code and modifying it throughout that code.

The Decorator design pattern takes a different approach. Instead of using external algorithms, this design pattern is all about using *wrapper* code to extend your core code.

The formal definition of the Decorator pattern from the GoF book (*Design Patterns: Elements of Reusable Object-Oriented Software*, 1995, Pearson Education, Inc. Publishing as Pearson Addison Wesley) says you can, "Attach additional responsibilities to an object dynamically. Decorators provide a flexible alternative to subclassing for extending functionality."

This design pattern is called Decorator but that seems to imply optional frills. A better name for this pattern might be the "Augmentor" or "Extender" pattern because that's what it allows you to do: augment or extend a class dynamically at runtime. However, as you see in this chapter, the term *Decorator* does apply once you understand the concept of "closed for modification, open for extension." When you use wrapper code to *extend* your core functionality and you don't need to modify that core functionality, you are essentially decorating the code.

Here's how it works. You might start with a core computer, like the one illustrated in Figure 3-1.

Figure 3-1:
You start with a core computer.

```
Computer
            description()
```

When you call the `description` method in this example, you get a return value of `You're getting a computer`. Now let's say you want to add more hardware — a disk, for example. In this case, you can add a wrapper as shown in Figure 3-2.

Figure 3-2:
Next, you add a disk drive.

```
Computer
            description()

Disk
            description()
```

Now when you call the wrapper's `description` method, it calls the `computer` object's `description` method to get the string `You're getting a computer` and adds `and a disk` to that string to give you `You're getting a computer and a disk`.

If you want to add more to the computer, you just place it in another wrapper, such as a Monitor wrapper, as shown in Figure 3-3.

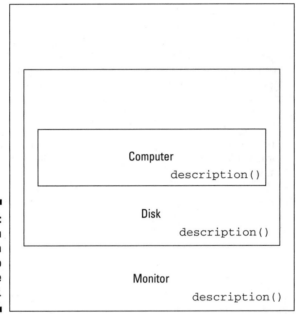

Figure 3-3:
Finally, you add a monitor to the computer.

Now when you call the resulting object's `description` method, the following occurs in this order:

1. The object's `description` method calls the `Disk` wrapper's `description` method.

2. The `Disk` wrapper's `description` method calls the `computer` object's `description` method.

3. The `computer` object's `description` method returns the text `You're getting a computer and a disk`.

4. The `Monitor` wrapper's `description` object then adds `and a monitor` to give you the resulting final string, `You're getting a computer and a disk and a monitor`.

Alright, let's see what this looks like in code.

Putting the Decorator Pattern to Work

You can start slinging some code by creating the core component, which is the computer in this example. Here's what that looks like — note that the description method just returns the plain text, computer.

```
public class Computer
{
  public Computer()
  {
  }

  public String description()
  {
    return "computer";
  }
}
```

Alright, that's the core component: the computer itself. Now how about creating some decorator classes? Such classes have to act as wrappers for the Computer class, which means that variables that can hold computer objects should also be able to hold objects that wrap computer objects. And one easy way to make sure that can happen is to extend the wrapper classes from the Computer class.

Creating a decorator

You might start by creating an abstract class that all Computer class wrappers have to extend (remember, an abstract class is one that can't be used to create objects directly, but must be inherited from to create a concrete class). Here's what that abstract class looks like:

```
public abstract class ComponentDecorator extends Computer
{
  public abstract String description();
}
```

This class, ComponentDecorator, has one abstract method, description. Because this class is abstract, you can't instantiate objects from it. It's meant to make sure that all wrappers are consistent — when developers extend this class, they'll have to provide their own version of the description method.

Adding a disk

Here's a concrete wrapper, `Disk`, which adds a hard disk to the core computer. This class starts by extending the `ComponentDecorator` abstract wrapper class:

```
public class Disk extends ComponentDecorator
{
    .
    .
    .
}
```

Because this is a wrapper class, it has to know what it's wrapping so you can pass a `computer` object to this class's constructor. The `Disk` wrapper will store the core `computer` object.

```
public class Disk extends ComponentDecorator
{
    Computer computer;

    public Disk(Computer c)
    {
        computer = c;
    }
    .
    .
    .
}
```

Now you've got to implement the `description` method. (You inherited the `description` method from the abstract `ComponentDecorator` class, which declares an abstract `description` method, so Java is going to insist you need to write the `description` method.) That method will call the core `computer` object's `description` method and add the text and a disk like this:

```
public class Disk extends ComponentDecorator
{
    Computer computer;

    public Disk(Computer c)
    {
        computer = c;
    }

    public String description()
    {
        return computer.description() + " and a disk";
    }
}
```

So if you wrap a `computer` object, whose `description` method returns the text `computer`, in a `Disk` wrapper, when the wrapper's `description` method adds the text `and a disk`, you end up with the total text `computer and a disk`. That's what you get from the `Disk` wrapper's `description` method at this point.

Adding a CD

Besides disks, you can also add CD drives to your computer purchase orders. Here's what the CD wrapper looks like — note that it adds `and a CD` to the return value from the wrapped object's `description` method:

```java
public class CD extends ComponentDecorator
{
  Computer computer;

  public CD(Computer c)
  {
    computer = c;
  }

  public String description()
  {
    return computer.description() + " and a CD";
  }
}
```

Adding a monitor

To add a monitor to the purchase order you have to make the monitor wrapper add the text `and a monitor` to the return value of the wrapped object's `description` method.

```java
public class Monitor extends ComponentDecorator
{
  Computer computer;

  public Monitor(Computer c)
  {
    computer = c;
  }

  public String description()
  {
    return computer.description() + " and a monitor";
  }
}
```

OK, that gives you all you need to start running some code. How about testing it out?

Testing it out

The best way to test out your computer component is to use a testing class, Test.java, that can be found in the downloadable code for this book. Test.java starts by creating a computer like this:

```
public class Test
{
  public static void main(String args[])
  {
    Computer computer = new Computer();
      .
      .
      .
  }
}
```

Then the code wraps that computer in a wrapper that adds a hard disk.

```
public class Test
{
  public static void main(String args[])
  {
    Computer computer = new Computer();

    computer = new Disk(computer);
      .
      .
      .
  }
}
```

Now let's add a monitor.

```
public class Test
{
  public static void main(String args[])
  {
    Computer computer = new Computer();

    computer = new Disk(computer);
    computer = new Monitor(computer);
      .
      .
      .
  }
}
```

Then, you might as well add not just one CD drive, but two — cost is no consideration here. Finally, you can display the resulting wrapped computer's full configuration by calling the computer's final `description` method.

```java
public class Test
{
  public static void main(String args[])
  {
    Computer computer = new Computer();

    computer = new Disk(computer);
    computer = new Monitor(computer);
    computer = new CD(computer);
    computer = new CD(computer);

    System.out.println("You're getting a " + computer.description()
      + ".");
  }
}
```

Java stream classes are decorators

You already know about decorator classes if you've ever worked with the file system in Java. That's how Java structures its file system classes — as decorators. Do you want to read data in a buffered way? You might take a look at a basic file-reading object, an `InputStream` object — but there's no accessible buffering there. So you might wrap an `InputStream` object inside a `FilterInputStream` object, and then wrap that in a `BufferedInputStream` object. The final wrapper, `BufferedInputStream`, will give you the buffering you want. Here's the class hierarchy:

```
java.lang.Object
|_java.io.InputStream
    |_java.io.FilterInput
  Stream
          |_java.io.Buffered
InputStream
```

And there you go; a `BufferedInputStream` object buffers what it gets from the objects it's wrapped, which in this case is a `FilterInputStream` object, which in turn wraps an `InputStream` object. That's the Decorator pattern at work, pure and simple. Here's what the Java 1.5 documents on `FilterInputStream` have to say — note how this description says "Decorator" in just about every line:

"A `FilterInputStream` contains some other input stream, which it uses as its basic source of data, possibly transforming the data along the way or providing additional functionality. The class `FilterInputStream` itself simply overrides all methods of `InputStream` with versions that pass all requests to the contained input stream. Subclasses of `FilterInputStream` may further override some of these methods and may also provide additional methods and fields."

And there you go. When you run this code, you get the fully extended computer model.

```
You're getting a computer and a disk and a monitor and a CD and a CD.
```

Not bad. You were able to extend the core object simply by wrapping it in various decorator wrappers, avoiding modification of the core code. Each successive wrapper called the description method of the object it wrapped in this case and added something to it. That's how you use the Decorator design pattern.

Improving the New Operator with the Factory Pattern

Here, in your capacity of highly paid, hotshot, design pattern pro for MegaGigaCo, you're creating a new database connection object. Behold the new operator at work, creating an object in a Java application:

```
Connection connection = new OracleConnection();
```

Not bad, you think, after finishing the coding for your OracleConnection class. Now you can connect to Oracle databases.

"But," wails the MegaGigaCo CEO, "what about connecting to Microsoft's SQL Server?"

"Alright," you say, "calm down. Let me think about this." You go off to lunch and then return to find the CEO and board of directors waiting anxiously in your office and asking, "Is it done yet?"

You get to work and create a new database connection class, SqlServerConnection. And you're able to create objects of this new class like this:

```
Connection connection = new SqlServerConnection();
```

"Great!" cries the CEO. "Um, what about connecting to MySQL? We want to make that the default connection." Jeez, you think. But you set to work, and presently, you get the useful MySqlConnection put together — and presto, now you can connect to MySQL databases.

```
Connection connection = new MySqlConnection();
```

But now you've got three different kinds of connections to make: Oracle, SQL Server, and MySQL. So you might start to adapt your code to make a connection based on the value in a variable named type: `"Oracle"`, `"SQL Server"`, or anything else (which results in the default connection to MySQL).

```
Connection connection;

if (type.equals("Oracle")){
  connection= new OracleConnection();
}
else if (type.equals("SQL Server")){
  connection = new SqlServerConnection();
}
else {
  connection = new MySqlConnection();
}
```

That's all fine, you think, but there are about 200 places in your code where you need to create a database connection. So maybe it's time to put this code into a method, `createConnection`, and pass the type of connection you want to that method as follows:

```
public Connection createConnection(String type)
{

  .
  .
  .
}
```

You can return the correct connection object, depending on what type of connection is required:

```
public Connection createConnection(String type)
{
  if (type.equals("Oracle")){
    return new OracleConnection();
  }
  else if (type.equals("SQL Server")){
    return new SqlServerConnection();
  }
  else {
    return new MySqlConnection();
  }
}
```

Bingo, you think. What could go wrong with that? "Bad news," cries the CEO, running into your office suddenly. "We need to rework your code to handle secure connections to all database servers as well! The board of our Western division is demanding it."

You push the CEO out of your office and start to think. All this code is starting to change a lot. Your new method, `createConnection`, is part of your core code, and it's the part you're editing the most.

In Chapter 2 of this book, you will find this valuable design insight: "Separate the parts of your code that will change the most from the rest of your application. And always try to reuse those parts as much as possible."

Maybe it's time to start thinking about separating out the part of the code that's changing so much — the `connection` object creation part — and encapsulating it in its own object. And that object is a *factory* object — it's a factory, written in code, for the creation of `connection` objects.

So how did you get here? Here's the trail of bread crumbs:

1. You started off by using the `new` operator to create `OracleConnection` objects.

2. Then you used the `new` operator to create `SqlServerConnection` objects, followed by `MySqlConnection` objects. In other words, you were using the `new` operator to instantiate many different concrete classes, and the code that did so was becoming larger and had to be replicated in many places.

3. Then you factored that code out into a method.

4. Because the code was still changing quickly, it turned out to be best to encapsulate the code out into a `factory` object. In that way, you were able to separate out the changeable code and leave the core code closed for modification.

All of which is to say — the `new` operator is fine as far as it goes, but when your object creation code changes a lot, it's time to think about factoring it out into `factory` objects.

Building Your First Factory

Lots of programmers know how `factory` objects work — or think they do. The idea, they think, is simply that you have an object that creates other objects. That's the way `factory` objects are usually created and used, but there's a little more to it than that. I look at the popular way of creating `factory` objects first, then take a look at the strict GoF definition, which is a little different, and a little more flexible.

Creating the factory

The first factory example, `FirstFactory`, does things the commonly understood way. The `FirstFactory` class encapsulates the `connection` object creation, and you can pass to it the type of connection you want to create (`"Oracle"`, `"SQL Server"`, or anything else). Here's how you might create an object factory using this class:

```
FirstFactory factory;

factory = new FirstFactory("Oracle");
```

Now you can use the new factory object to create `connection` objects like this with a factory method named `createConnection`.

```
FirstFactory factory;

factory = new FirstFactory("Oracle");

Connection connection = factory.createConnection();
```

That's the idea, and you've probably seen how this works in Java, as when you create `XMLReader` objects (discussed later in this chapter). How do you create the `FirstFactory` class? To start, save the type of the database you're connecting to, which is passed to the `FirstFactory` class's constructor.

```
public class FirstFactory
{
  protected String type;

  public FirstFactory(String t)
  {
    type = t;
  }
    .
    .
    .
}
```

The `FirstFactory` class exposes the public method `createConnection` which is what actually creates the objects. Here's where the object-creation code that changes a lot goes — all you have to do is to check which type of object you should be creating (`OracleConnection`, `SqlServerConnection`, or `MySqlConnection`) and then create it.

```
public class FirstFactory
{
  protected String type;

  public FirstFactory(String t)
  {
    type = t;
  }

  public Connection createConnection()
  {
    if (type.equals("Oracle")){
      return new OracleConnection();
    }
    else if (type.equals("SQL Server")){
      return new SqlServerConnection();
    }
    else {
      return new MySqlConnection();
    }
  }
}
```

There you go — you've got a factory class.

Creating the abstract Connection class

Remember that one of our objectives is to make sure that the core code doesn't have to be modified or has to be modified as little as possible. Bearing that in mind, take a look at this code that uses the connection object returned by our new factory object:

```
FirstFactory factory;

factory = new FirstFactory("Oracle");

Connection connection = factory.createConnection();

connection.setParams("username", "Steve");

connection.setParams("password", "Open the door!!!");

connection.initialize();

connection.open();
      .
      .
      .
```

As you see, the `connection` objects created by our factory are going to be used extensively in the code. To be able to use the same code for all the different types of `connection` objects we're going to return (for Oracle connections, MySQL connections, and so on), the code should be *polymorphic* — all `connection` objects should share the same interface or be derived from the same base class. That way, you'll be able to use the same variable for any created object.

In this case, I make `Connection` an abstract class so all the classes derived from it for the various connection types (`OracleConnection`, `MySqlConnection`, and so on) can use the same code after being created by the `FirstFactory` object. The `Connection` class will have just a constructor and a `description` method (which will return a description of the type of connection).

```
public abstract class Connection
{
  public Connection()
  {
  }

  public String description()
  {
    return "Generic";
  }
}
```

Okay, that looks good. Now that you've created the abstract base class for all concrete connection classes that will be created by our factory, how about creating those concrete classes?

You should derive all the objects your factory creates from the same base class or interface so that code that uses the objects it creates doesn't have to be modified for each new object type.

Creating the concrete connection classes

There are three concrete connection classes that `FirstFactory` can create, matching the connections the CEO wants: `OracleConnection`, `SqlServerConnection`, and `MySqlConnection`. As just discussed, each of these should be based on the abstract `Connection` class so they can be used in `Connection` variables after the `factory` object creates them. And each of them should return a description from the `description` method that indicates what kind of connection each connection is. Here's how the `OracleConnection` class looks in code:

```
public class OracleConnection extends Connection
{
  public OracleConnection()
  {
  }

  public String description()
  {
    return "Oracle";
  }
}
```

Here's the `SqlServerConnection` class — also based on the abstract `Connection` class:

```
public class SqlServerConnection extends Connection
{
  public SqlServerConnection()
  {
  }

  public String description()
  {
    return "SQL Server";
  }
}
```

And here's the `MySqlConnection` class, also based on the abstract `Connection` class, and like the others, with its own `description` method:

```
public class MySqlConnection extends Connection
{
  public MySqlConnection()
  {
  }

  public String description()
  {
    return "MySQL";
  }
}
```

Excellent — now you've got the factory class set up, as well as the classes that the factory uses to create objects. How about putting it to the test?

Testing it out

Everything's ready to go; all you need is a framework to test it in, `TestConnection.java`. You can start by creating a `factory` object which will create Oracle connections.

```
public class TestConnection
{
  public static void main(String args[])
  {
    FirstFactory factory;

    factory = new FirstFactory("Oracle");
              .
              .
              .

  }
}
```

As is usual for `factory` objects, you use a method of the `factory` object, `createConnection` in this case, to create objects. Because all objects created by this factory inherit from the `Connection` class, you can store whatever object the factory creates in a `Connection` variable.

```
public class TestConnection
{
  public static void main(String args[])
  {
    FirstFactory factory;

    factory = new FirstFactory("Oracle");

    Connection connection = factory.createConnection();
              .
              .
              .

  }
}
```

To check the `connection` object that's been created and make sure it's an Oracle `connection` object, just call its `description` method.

```
public class TestConnection
{
  public static void main(String args[])
  {
    FirstFactory factory;

    factory = new FirstFactory("Oracle");

    Connection connection = factory.createConnection();

    System.out.println("You're connecting with " +
      connection.description());
  }
}
```

What are the results? You should see the following message:

```
You're connecting with Oracle
```

Not bad; that's what you'd expect of most `factory` objects you usually come across.

In fact, Java comes stocked with various factories already, such as the `XMLReaderFactory` class, which lets you build `XMLReader` objects.

```
try {
    XMLReader myReader = XMLReaderFactory.createXMLReader();
} catch (SAXException e) {
    System.err.println(e.getMessage());
}
```

In Java, `XMLReaderFactory` is a *final class,* not designed for inheritance. A factory class is a factory class, and that's it. It's not designed to be extended. But the formal GoF Factory design pattern is somewhat different — it offers you more flexibility because before using GoF factories, you're *supposed* to extend them.

According to the GoF book, the Factory Method design pattern should "Define an interface for creating an object, but let subclasses decide which class to instantiate. Factory method lets a class defer instantiation to subclasses."

The key here is the part that says: "let the subclasses decide." So far, the factory classes you've seen here don't let the subclasses decide how to configure the factory — unless they simply inherit from it and override it, method by method.

The GoF Factory Method design pattern gives you more flexibility than the traditional object factory. The GoF way of doing things means that you define how factory methods should work and leave it up to subclassers to implement the actual factory.

Say that the Western division of MegaGigaCo suddenly calls and says that they don't like the `FirstFactory` class at all — they want to be able to create secure connections to the database server, not just standard connections. And that means they've been having to rewrite `FirstFactory` every time you change it, so that they can create secure database connections.

That's an issue for the developers — every time you update the `FirstFactory` class, the developers have to rewrite it and adapt it for their own use. They're calling to say they want more control over the process.

Fine, you say, that's what the GoF Factory Method design pattern is really all about — delegating control to subclassers. To see how this works, I change the way `connection` objects are created, using the GoF techniques that will make even MegaGigaCo's Western division happy.

Still unclear about when to use the GoF Factory Method design pattern? Consider the GoF Factory Method pattern when circumstances have gotten decentralized enough so that many programmers who subclass your factory class are overriding it so much that they're changing it substantially.

Creating a Factory the GoF Way

How do you "let the subclasses decide which class to instantiate" when creating an object factory? The way to do that is to define your factory as an abstract class or interface that has to be implemented by the subclasses that actually do the work by creating objects.

In other words, you at MegaGigaCo headquarters can create the specification for `factory` objects, and the actual implementation of those factories is up to those who subclass your specification. It all starts by creating that factory specification, and I do that with an abstract factory class.

Creating an abstract factory

Creating the abstract factory class is easy. This class will be called `ConnectionFactory`.

```
public abstract class ConnectionFactory
{
    .
    .
    .
}
```

Besides an empty constructor, the important method here is the factory method `createConnection`. I make this method abstract so that any sub-classes have to implement it. This method takes one argument — the type of connection you want to create.

```
public abstract class ConnectionFactory
{
    public ConnectionFactory()
    {
    }

    protected abstract Connection createConnection(String type);
}
```

And that's all you need — the specification for an object factory. Now the Western division will be happy because they can implement their own concrete factory classes from this abstract factory class.

Creating a concrete factory

You've flown out to the MegaGigaCo Western division to set them straight on this business of object creation. You explain, "I understand that you want to gain more control over object creation using your own factory methods."

"Yep," say the Western division programmers. "We want to be able to work with secure database connections. We've created some new classes, SecureOracleConnection, SecureSqlServerConnection, and SecureMySqlConnection to create secure connections."

"Okay," you say, "all you have to do is to extend the new abstract class I've named ConnectionFactory when you create your own object factory. Make sure you implement the createConnection method, or Java won't let you compile. Then it's up to you to write the code in the createConnection method to create objects of the new secure type that you want to use."

The Western division programmers say, "Hey, that's easy. We'll name our new concrete factory class that creates connection objects SecureFactory, and it'll extend your abstract ConnectionFactory class this way":

```
public class SecureFactory extends ConnectionFactory
{
       .
       .
       .
}
```

"Next," the Western division programmers say, "we just implement the createConnection class that the abstract ConnectionFactory class requires like this":

```
public class SecureFactory extends ConnectionFactory
{
    public Connection createConnection(String type)
    {
         .
         .
         .
    }
}
```

"Finally," the programmers say, "we just need to create objects from our own classes, the SecureOracleConnection, SecureSqlServerConnection, and SecureMySqlConnection classes, depending on the type passed to the createConnection method":

```
public class SecureFactory extends ConnectionFactory
{
  public Connection createConnection(String type)
  {
    if (type.equals("Oracle")){
      return new SecureOracleConnection();
    }
    else if (type.equals("SQL Server")){
      return new SecureSqlServerConnection();
    }
    else {
      return new SecureMySqlConnection();
    }
  }
}
```

"Simple!" they say.

And it is simple. The difference between the usual way of creating object factories and the GoF way is that the GoF way provides more of a specification for a factory and lets subclassers handle the details.

Creating the secure connection classes

To get this GoF Factory Method example off the ground, you need concrete classes for the new secure connection object factory to create, the SecureOracleConnection, SecureSqlServerConnection, and SecureMySqlConnection classes. They're easy to create — start with the SecureOracleConnection class, whose description method returns the text "Oracle secure".

```
public class SecureOracleConnection extends Connection
{
  public SecureOracleConnection()
  {
  }

  public String description()
  {
    return "Oracle secure";
  }
}
```

The `SecureSqlServerConnection` class's `description` method returns the text `"SQL Server secure"`.

```
public class SecureSqlServerConnection extends Connection
{
  public SecureSqlServerConnection()
  {
  }

  public String description()
  {
    return "SQL Server secure";
  }
}
```

And the `SecureMySqlConnection` class's `description` method returns `"MySQL secure"`.

```
public class SecureMySqlConnection extends Connection
{
  public SecureMySqlConnection()
  {
  }

  public String description()
  {
    return "MySQL secure";
  }
}
```

That completes the code for this example — the next step is to see if it'll prove itself.

Testing it out

Test your code with `TestFactory.java`; this creates a `SecureFactory` object factory and uses it to create a `SecureOracleConnection` object. You create the factory as follows:

```
public class TestFactory
{
  public static void main(String args[])
  {
    SecureFactory factory;

    factory = new SecureFactory();
```

```
         .
         .
         .
      }
   }
```

Then all you've got to do is use the factory's `createConnection` method to create a new secure connection to a database server like Oracle and use the created `connection` object to verify that you're now building secure connections, as the Western division wanted to do.

```
public class TestFactory
{
  public static void main(String args[])
  {
    SecureFactory factory;

    factory = new SecureFactory();

    Connection connection = factory.createConnection("Oracle");

    System.out.println("You're connecting with " +
      connection.description());
  }
}
```

When you run this, you get, as expected, this text, indicating that you used a secure Oracle connection:

```
You're connecting with Oracle secure
```

The result is just what you'd get from the `FirstFactory` example discussed earlier in this chapter, except that now, you've let the Western division programmers implement their own version of your factory. You set the factory specification by creating an abstract class or interface that subclassers have to use, and they build the actual concrete factory that can create objects. No longer does a single concrete `factory` object instantiate your objects — a set of subclasses does the work.

Chapter 4

Watch What's Going On with the Observer and Chain of Responsibility Patterns

*T*he big boss comes into your office and says, "Someone's been editing the data in our central database — why wasn't I informed?"

"How's that?" you ask. "You want to be informed of *every* edit that happens to the data?" You know the boss is new on the job, but this is something even more clueless than you'd expected.

"That's right," the boss says. "I want personal notification each time a record is changed in the database. I want to keep an eye on what goes on around here."

"You mean, like a memo?"

"Right."

"Hmm," you say. "I think I have a better idea. How about I use the Observer design pattern and register you as a database observer?"

"Huh?" the boss asks.

"You'll be notified each time the database is modified," you say. "No memos needed. It'll all be done automatically, in code."

"That's all I ask," the boss says, leaving.

You smile to yourself as you turn to the code, wondering how happy the boss is going to be with about 200,000 notifications a day. But, by using the Observer design pattern, the coding won't be hard to set up.

This chapter is about keeping your objects in the know when something's happened and passing the word to notify either a set or a whole chain of objects. There are two design patterns coming up in this chapter — the Observer design pattern, and the Chain of Responsibility design pattern.

The Observer design pattern lets several observer objects be notified when a subject object is changed in some way. Each observer registers with the subject, and when a change occurs, the subject notifies them all. Each of the observers is notified in parallel (that is, at the same time).

The Chain of Responsibility design pattern also lets you notify objects of a change, but this time, the objects are connected in a chain — that is, in series. The notification goes from one object to the next until an object is found that can handle the notification.

Notifying Observers with the Observer Pattern

The boss wants to be notified each time a change is made to the company's database. And, come to think of it, you might as well archive all those changes as well. Not only that, but the client who's making the changes should be notified of the success or failure of her changes as well.

So now that you've got a set of "observers" that needs to know what's going on, it makes sense to start thinking in terms of the Observer pattern, which lets a subject (the database) notify a set of observers (the archive, the boss, and the client) of changes or events.

The Observer design pattern is all about sending notifications to update a set of objects. You can add new observer objects at runtime and remove them as well. When an event occurs, all registered observers are notified.

The Gang of Four book (*Design Patterns: Elements of Reusable Object-Oriented Software*, 1995, Pearson Education, Inc. Publishing as Pearson Addison Wesley) says that the Observer design pattern should "Define a one-to-many dependency between objects so that when one object changes state, all its dependents are notified and updated automatically."

Here's how it works. An observer can register with the subject as shown in Figure 4-1.

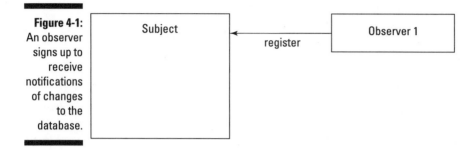

Figure 4-1:
An observer signs up to receive notifications of changes to the database.

The server stores the information that observer has registered. Then another observer, Observer 2, registers as well (see Figure 4-2).

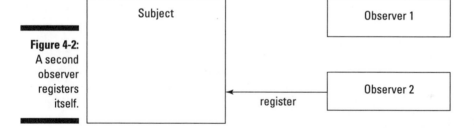

Figure 4-2:
A second observer registers itself.

At this point, the subject (database) is keeping track of two observers. When an event occurs, the subject notifies both observers as shown in Figure 4-3.

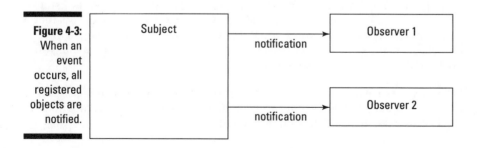

Figure 4-3:
When an event occurs, all registered objects are notified.

At any time, an observer, such as Observer 1, can *unregister* (ask to stop receiving notifications — for example, it may be shutting down) with the subject, as shown in Figure 4-4.

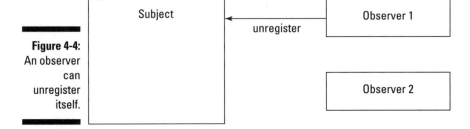

Figure 4-4:
An observer
can
unregister
itself.

Now that Observer 1 is no longer registered, it no longer receives notifications (see Figure 4-5).

Figure 4-5:
Notifica-
tions are
no longer
sent to the
unregistered
observer.

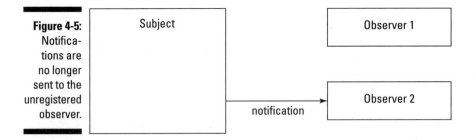

However, Observer 1 can register again at any time and be added to the subject's internal lists of observers once again.

You should consider the Observer design pattern when, as with event listeners in Java, you have an object that can cause events to occur — events that you want other objects to know about. Instead of writing everything in one monolithic class, consider breaking control out into a set of objects that will be notified when an event occurs.

In this example, when a record is edited, the database informs all registered observers of the change — that's the whole idea behind this pattern. Time to start coding this to get it down in black and white.

The Observer pattern in Java

Java implements this design pattern to some extent by using listeners that listen for user interface events. Want to create a button in your application? Just make sure you connect a listener to it to handle button events.

```
JButton button = new JButton("Check
        Spelling");
JTextField text = new JTextField(30);

public void init()
{
  Container contentPane =
        getContentPane();

  contentPane.setLayout(new
        FlowLayout());
  contentPane.add(button);
```

```
  contentPane.add(text);

  button.addActionListener(new
        ActionListener()
  {
    public void
        actionPerformed(ActionEvent
        event) {
      text.setText("Good job.");
    }
  });
}
```

In the Java model, you can add as many listeners (observers) as you like, and that's the way it works with the loose coupling of the Observer design pattern.

Creating a subject interface

When you implement a design pattern, it's often a good idea to start by creating an interface to make sure that the objects you create will adhere to the pattern you're trying to use — especially if multiple objects are involved. Implementing that interface — programming to an interface as it's called — keeps your code in line and usually keeps things clearer.

When you're putting the Observer pattern into code, set up an interface or abstract class for the observers; you'll usually have multiple observers, and you have to keep the methods they implement consistent.

In this example, I also need to set up an interface for the subject, which is what the observers watch; the Subject interface lists the methods subjects must implement. I put a registerObserver method here so that the subject can keep track of observers that want to be registered. Besides registering observers, you should have some way to get rid of them, so I add a removeObserver method. And there's a notifyObservers method that will notify the observers of some change.

```
public interface Subject
{
  public void registerObserver(Observer o);
  public void removeObserver(Observer o);
  public void notifyObservers();
}
```

This interface lists the methods that subjects like the database system should implement. Next up: the interface for the observers.

Creating an observer interface

Building the Observer interface, implemented by the observers to enable them to get notifications, is simple. All you need is a method that will be called when a new notification is ready, and I'll call that method update. In this example, you pass the database operation that was performed (such as "edit", "delete", "create" and so on) and the record that was changed as strings to the update method.

```
public interface Observer
{
  public void update(String operation, String record);
}
```

When observers implement the update method, the subject is able to pass them the record that's been affected and the operation that was performed.

Okay, we're good to go. It's time to create the Database subject that is going to keep track of the observers and notify them when there's been a change.

Creating a subject

The subject has to let observers register and has to notify them when an event occurs. According to the Subject interface, the three methods a subject has to implement in these examples are: registerObserver, removeObserver, and notifyObservers. That's what the Database class does in this example.

To keep track of the observers, I will use a Java vector named observers, created in the Database constructor. (The type specifier here, <Observer>, is for Java 1.5 or later and indicates that each observer object implements the Observer interface; if you're using an earlier version of Java, omit the type specifier.)

```java
import java.util.*;

public class Database implements Subject
{
  private Vector<Observer> observers;

  public Database()
  {
    observers = new Vector<Observer>();
  }
        .
        .
        .
}
```

When you use a vector, keeping track of observers is simple. When an observer wants to register, it calls the subject's registerObserver method, passing itself as an object. The subject — an object of our Database class — just has to add that observer to the observers vector in the registerObserver method, using the Vector class's add method.

```java
import java.util.*;

public class Database implements Subject
{
  private Vector<Observer> observers;

  public Database()
  {
    observers = new Vector<Observer>();
  }

  public void registerObserver(Observer o)
  {
    observers.add(o);
  }
        .
        .
        .
}
```

How about removing an observer from the observers vector? No problem. When you want to remove an object from a vector, you can use the vector's remove method; here's how that works in the Database class's removeObserver method:

```java
import java.util.*;

public class Database implements Subject
```

```
{
  private Vector<Observer> observers;

  public Database()
  {
    observers = new Vector<Observer>();
  }

  public void registerObserver(Observer o)
  {
    observers.add(o);
  }

  public void removeObserver(Observer o)
  {
    observers.remove(o);
  }
      .
      .
      .
}
```

When the user actually does something with the database — deletes a record, for example — he calls the Database class's editRecord method. For example, to delete record 1, you might call this method like this:

```
database.editRecord("delete", "record 1");
```

Here's what the editRecord method looks like: When this method is called, you pass it the database operation you want to perform and the record you want to work on, both as strings in this example. Those strings are stored so they can be passed on to the observers. After the strings are stored, the notifyObservers method, coming up next, is called to notify all observers.

```
import java.util.*;

public class Database implements Subject
{
  private Vector<Observer> observers;
  private String operation;
  private String record;

  public Database()
  {
    observers = new Vector<Observer>();
  }
      .
      .
      .
  public void editRecord(String operation, String record)
```

```
  {
    this.operation = operation;
    this.record = record;
    notifyObservers();
  }
}
```

Here's the meat of the code, the part that notifies each observer that there's been a change: the notifyObservers method. Each observer implements this example's Observer interface — which means it has an update method — so notifyObservers just has to loop over all registered observers in the observers vector, calling each one's update method with the database operation and affected record.

```
import java.util.*;

public class Database implements Subject
{
  private Vector<Observer> observers;
  private String operation;
  private String record;

    .
    .
    .

  public void notifyObservers()
  {
    for (int loopIndex = 0; loopIndex < observers.size(); loopIndex++) {
      Observer observer = (Observer)observers.get(loopIndex);
      observer.update(operation, record);
    }
  }

  public void editRecord(String operation, String record)
  {
    this.operation = operation;
    this.record = record;
    notifyObservers();
  }
}
```

That's all you need for Database.java, the subject in this example. The subject will let observers register themselves, unregister themselves, and get notified when a database record has been edited (which you do with the Database class's editRecord method). All that's left to do to get this show on the road is to create the observers themselves.

Creating observers

This example has three observers — the archive for data backup, the client who's actually doing the work on the database, and the boss, who wants to be notified of every change. To create an observer, you just have to implement the `Observer` interface you've created, which has only one method, `update`. Here's what creating an observer for the archives, which I'll call the `Archiver` class, looks like:

```
public class Archiver implements Observer
{
  public Archiver()
  {
  }

  public void update(String operation, String record)
  {

      .
      .
      .
  }
}
```

The database record and the editing operation are passed as strings to the `update` method. When called, the `update` method displays that information on the screen.

```
public class Archiver implements Observer
{
  public Archiver()
  {
  }

  public void update(String operation, String record)
  {
     System.out.println("The archiver says a " + operation +
       " operation was performed on " + record);
  }
}
```

When the `update` method is called, then, you're going to see a message something like this, which gives the name of the observer that was notified by the subject:

```
The archiver says a delete operation was performed on record 1
```

The observer for the client — the `Client` class — looks like this:

```
public class Client implements Observer
{
  public Client()
  {
  }

  public void update(String operation, String record)
```

```
  {
    System.out.println("The client says a " + operation +
      " operation was performed on " + record);
  }
}
```

And here's the `observer` class for the boss, the `Boss` class:

```
public class Boss implements Observer
{
  public Boss()
  {
  }

  public void update(String operation, String record)
  {
    System.out.println("The boss says a " + operation +
      " operation was performed on " + record);
  }
}
```

You now have a subject (`Database.java`) and three observers (`Archiver.java`, `Client.java`, and `Boss.java`).

Testing the Database observers

Brilliant! You're ready to test the database and its observers. The test harness here is called `TestObserver.java`, and the idea is to create a `Database` object, register the observers with that object, and see if they catch edits to the database.

The inspiration here is loose coupling. (For more on this critical concept, check out the sidebar "Loose coupling beats a monolith" in this chapter.) No more information is traded than need be, keeping the data space chatter down to a minimum. And the observers aren't locked into the core code because you're using a "has-a" relationship to store observer objects in the subject code. (For more on "has-a" relationships, turn to Chapter 2.)

Here it goes. You start by creating a `Database` object as shown in the following:

```
public class TestObserver
{
  public static void main(String args[])
  {
    Database database = new Database();
      .
      .
      .
  }
}
```

And you need the three observers.

```
public class TestObserver
{
  public static void main(String args[])
  {
    Database database = new Database();
    Archiver archiver = new Archiver();
    Client client = new Client();
    Boss boss = new Boss();
      .
      .
      .
  }
}
```

You've got the subject and the observers. Now you've got to register the observers with the subject, which you do with the Database class's registerObserver method. You pass the observer to register to that method this way:

```
public class TestObserver
{
  public static void main(String args[])
  {
    Database database = new Database();
    Archiver archiver = new Archiver();
    Client client = new Client();
    Boss boss = new Boss();

    database.registerObserver(archiver);
    database.registerObserver(client);
    database.registerObserver(boss);
      .
      .
      .
  }
}
```

Alright, the observers are connected to the subject. Theoretically, when something happens to the database, all three observers will be notified, and they'll display a message. Is this going to work? There's only one way to find out. You can make a change to the database with the Database class's editRecord method, which stores the operation you want to perform and the record you want to perform it on, and notifies the waiting observers.

In this case, I'm going to perform a delete operation on record 1 in the database:

```
public class TestObserver
{
  public static void main(String args[])
  {
    Database database = new Database();
    Archiver archiver = new Archiver();
    Client client = new Client();
    Boss boss = new Boss();

    database.registerObserver(archiver);
    database.registerObserver(client);
    database.registerObserver(boss);
    database.editRecord("delete", "record 1");
  }
}
```

Compile the code and run it; you should see the following:

```
The boss says a delete operation was performed on record 1
The client says a delete operation was performed on record 1
The archiver says a delete operation was performed on record 1
```

Excellent. All the observers were notified, which is just what you want.

That's an implementation of the Observer design pattern. It's more flexible than hard coding everything into one unbreakable block and allows you to add or remove observers at runtime. It couples your objects loosely, which is something you should strive for, and builds composite objects using "has-a" relationships.

Loose coupling beats a monolith

Both the design patterns discussed in this chapter are about sending notifications to other objects. The Observer and Chain of Responsibility design patterns implement what's called *loose coupling* — connecting objects through notifications rather than hard coding a connection.

When you hard code command handling throughout a single class, you can end up with a large, monolithic class that's hard to debug or even understand. By breaking things out into encapsulated objects that communicate no more than they need to — using simple notifications — you can often gain a great deal of flexibility and robustness. By working with more self-contained objects, you're able to debug and develop those semi-independent objects easier, making agile development easier. The design insight here is that loose coupling between objects, rather than simply extending objects by making them do more than they were meant to do, is good design policy.

For maximal flexibility, go for loose coupling when it comes to information flow, not tight coupling. Think of loose coupling as just another part of OOP (object-oriented programming) encapsulation when it comes to application design.

Using Java's Observer Interface and Observable Class

Java already comes with some built-in support for creating observer-based code, but, as you're going to see, it's not as flexible as the code discussed earlier in this chapter. Java's support here is based on the `Observer` interface and the `Observable` class.

Watching with the Observer interface

The `Observer` interface is what you create observers with. This interface has just one method, `update`, that looks like this:

```
void update(Observable o, Object arg)
```

This is a lot like the observers discussed in the previous section of this chapter — everything there centers around the observer's `update` method, which is called when the observer is notified of a change.

There's a difference here — this update method is passed an `Observable` object and a generic object (when you implement the Observer design pattern from scratch, you can set what's passed to your observers). You can specify what generic object you want passed to the observers by passing that object to the `Observable` class's `notifyObservers` method (coming up shortly), but you don't have any choice about passing the `Observable` object. In the examples in the previous section of this chapter, the `Observable` object is the `Database` object, and each observer will be able to interrogate that object to find out what record was edited, and how.

That brings up a potential problem issue. Note that the entire subject is passed to each observer every time the observers need to be updated. The object is passed by reference, as usual for objects in Java, so even if the `Database` object is huge, you don't have to worry about running out of memory; the `Database` object itself isn't passed, but a reference to it is. But that means that each observer has direct access to the subject object, and so can potentially change the subject object or the data in it, as well as potentially causing deadlock issues with shared resources. That's not what you'd call loose coupling; as a general design insight, it's best to trade only the information you need to trade.

Notifying with the Observable class

The Java `Observable` class is what you create subjects with; more specifically, you extend this class to create subjects. This class features some of the following built-in methods:

- ✔ `void addObserver(Observer o)`   Adds an observer to the internally stored set of registered observers for this subject.

- ✔ `protected void clearChanged()`   Clears the internal changed flag, meaning that no changes are waiting to be passed to the observers.

- ✔ `int countObservers()`   Returns the number of observers currently registered for this subject.

- ✔ `void deleteObserver(Observer o)`   Removes a registered observer from the internally stored set of observers for this subject.

- ✔ `void deleteObservers()`   Removes all registered observers for this subject; there will be no registered observers when the call returns.

- ✔ `boolean hasChanged()`   Returns true if the subject has changed.

- ✔ `void notifyObservers()`   Notifies all registered observers that this object has changed by calling their update methods, if there has been a change. You can indicate that there has been a change by calling the `setChanged` method.

- ✔ `void notifyObservers(Object arg)`   Notifies all registered observers that this object has changed and passes the given object to them by calling their update methods, if there has been a change. You can indicate that there has been a change by calling the `setChanged` method.

- ✔ `protected void setChanged()`   Sets this subject object as having been changed. Call this before calling `notifyObservers`, or `notify Observers` will not do anything.

Note that when you use a subject that extends the `Observable` class, you have to call the `setChanged` method before calling `notifyObservers`. If you don't call `setChanged` first, `notifyObservers` won't do anything.

When the `update` method of each observer is called, how do you actually pass data on to those `observers`? There are two ways, corresponding to the two objects the `update` method is called with, the `Observable` object itself, and another object you can (optionally) specify:

```
void update(Observable o, Object arg)
```

You can either build in getter/setter methods into the `Observable` object, or put together an object with all the data you want to send to observers and pass that object to the `notifyObservers` method; that object will then be passed as the second argument to the `update` method of the observers. I'm going to modify the database example to use Java's `Observer/Observable` as an example, and I'll use the first technique — adding getter/setter methods to the Observable object — here.

Creating the Observable object

To create a subject, you extend the `Observable` class, so here's how I create the new version of the `Database` class:

```
import java.util.Observable;
import java.util.Observer;

public class Database extends Observable
{
  public Database()
  {
  }

        .

        .

        .

}
```

To let users make changes to the database, I add the `editRecord` method, which is passed both the operation to perform and the record in question (passed as strings to make the code easier). The `editRecord` method stores the operation and record, then calls the `setChanged` and `notifyObservers` methods to pass that new data along to the observers.

```
import java.util.Observable;
import java.util.Observer;

public class Database extends Observable
{
  private String operation;
  private String record;

  public Database()
  {
  }

  public void editRecord(String operation, String record)
  {
```

```
      this.operation = operation;
      this.record = record;
      setChanged();
      notifyObservers();
   }
      .
      .
      .
 }
```

When the observers are called, they're passed the Database object, so I add getter methods to let code retrieve the database operation and affected record from that object.

```java
import java.util.Observable;
import java.util.Observer;

public class Database extends Observable
{
  private String operation;
  private String record;

  public Database()
  {
  }

  public void editRecord(String operation, String record)
  {
    this.operation = operation;
    this.record = record;
    setChanged();
    notifyObservers();
  }

  public String getRecord()
  {
    return record;
  }

  public String getOperation()
  {
    return operation;
  }
}
```

So far so good; you've built the subject, complete with the editRecord method that you use to work with the database, and getter methods to allow access to information about what's going on in the database. Now you need to build the observers.

Creating the Observer objects

To implement the `Archiver`, `Client`, and `Boss` observers, you implement the `java.util.Observer` interface, as here in the `Archiver` class:

```
import java.util.Observer;

public class Archiver implements Observer
{
    .
    .
    .
}
```

I also add an empty constructor and implement the `update` method from the `Observer` interface.

```
import java.util.Observer;

public class Archiver implements Observer
{

    public Archiver()
    {
    }

    public void update(Observable obs, Object record)
    {
        .
        .
        .
    }
}
```

Each observer's `update` method is passed the subject `Database` object and an optional, unused object. The `Database` object has been written to include `getter` methods for the operation the user is performing and the record he or she is working on, so all you have to do in this example in each observer is get that information and display it.

```
import java.util.Observer;

public class Archiver implements Observer
{

    public Archiver()
    {
    }
```

```
public void update(Observable obs, Object record)
{
  System.out.println("The archiver says a " +
    ((Database)obs).getOperation() +
    " operation was performed on " + ((Database)obs).getRecord());
}
}
```

Same goes for the Boss class, which will also grab the data about what the user did and display it.

```
import java.util.Observer;

public class Boss implements Observer
{

  public Boss()
  {
  }

  public void update(Observable obs, Object record)
  {
    System.out.println("The boss says a " +
      ((Database)obs).getOperation() +
      " operation was performed on " + ((Database)obs).getRecord());
  }
}
```

And the Client class also grabs that information and displays it.

```
import java.util.Observer;

public class Client implements Observer
{

  public Client()
  {
  }

  public void update(Observable obs, Object record)
  {
    System.out.println("The client says a " +
      ((Database)obs).getOperation() +
      " operation was performed on " + ((Database)obs).getRecord());
  }
}
```

Bingo, you're set — you've created all three observers. All that remains is to create your objects, test them, and connect them in an observer/observable relationship.

Testing the Observable code

The file `TestObservable.java` in the downloadable code for the book (see the Introduction for the Web address where you can download this) is a test harness that creates `Database` (subject) and `Archiver`, `Client`, and `Boss` (observer) objects and connects them. It starts by creating all the necessary objects.

```java
public class TestObservable
{
  public static void main(String args[])
  {
    Database database = new Database();

    Archiver archiver = new Archiver();
    Client client = new Client();
    Boss boss = new Boss();
        .
        .
        .

  }
}
```

To add an observer to an `Observable` object, you use the `Observable` class's `addObserver` method, which is much like the `addListener` method used when working with UI (user interface) elements. Here's how to add the `archiver`, `client`, and `boss` objects as observers of the database object:

```java
public class TestObservable
{
  public static void main(String args[])
  {
    Database database = new Database();

    Archiver archiver = new Archiver();
    Client client = new Client();
    Boss boss = new Boss();

    database.addObserver(archiver);
    database.addObserver(client);
    database.addObserver(boss);
        .
        .
        .

  }
}
```

That connects the observer objects to the `observable` object. To make something happen, just call the `Database` class's `editRecord` method to make a change in the database, and the Database then notifies the observers:

```
public class TestObservable
{
  public static void main(String args[])
  {
    Database database = new Database();

    Archiver archiver = new Archiver();
    Client client = new Client();
    Boss boss = new Boss();

    database.addObserver(archiver);
    database.addObserver(client);
    database.addObserver(boss);

    database.editRecord("delete", "record 1");
  }
}
```

Compile and run this test harness; you'll see that each observer is notified of the change with the following messages:

```
The boss says a delete operation was performed on record 1
The client says a delete operation was performed on record 1
The archiver says a delete operation was performed on record 1
```

Do-it-yourself Observables

The Observable code you tested with `TestObservable.java` works. Great, right? However, I suggest that if you want to do this, you should write it yourself. The `Observable` class is a concrete class, and that limits your flexibility. You can't change what's passed to observers, and you can't let subclasses implement their own versions of the `Observable` methods unless they want to override those methods — in which case, why are you using the `Observable` class at all?

Because `Observable` is a class, you have to extend it in your own code, and that's a problem because Java doesn't allow multiple inheritance — if you subclass `Observable`, you can't subclass from your own classes. That wipes out your use of inheritance in your application, which is too big a price to pay. If `Observable` were an interface, the story might be different, but it's a concrete class.

And on top of that, `Observable` hides important methods like `setChanged` that you might have reasonable reasons to use without having to subclass the `Observable` class. So although `Observable` works, you should consider it only a lightweight implementation of the Observer pattern.

Using the Chain of Responsibility Pattern

Here's another pattern that's all about notifying other objects when something's happened: the Chain of Responsibility design pattern. This pattern is all about connecting objects in a chain of notification; as a notification travels down the chain, it's handled by the first object that is set up to deal with the particular notification.

The Observer pattern notifies observers in parallel fashion as shown in Figure 4-6:

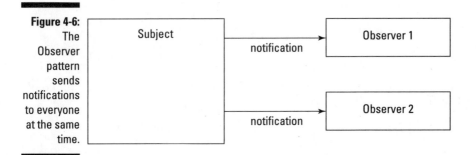

Figure 4-6: The Observer pattern sends notifications to everyone at the same time.

But the Chain of Responsibility pattern notifies objects in series, along a chain as illustrated in Figure 4-7:

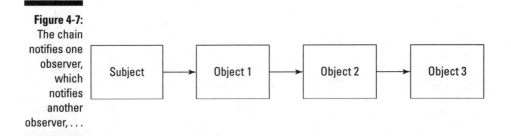

Figure 4-7: The chain notifies one observer, which notifies another observer, . . .

The first object in the chain that can deal with the notification handles it, and any following objects aren't notified.

The GoF book says that the Chain of Responsibility design pattern should "Avoid coupling the sender of a request to its receiver by giving more than one object a chance to handle the request. Chain the receiving objects and pass the request along the chain until an object handles it."

You use this pattern when not all your observers are created equal. For example, say that you have a layered application with a set chain of command for events — a mouse event may originate in a particular control, then bubble up to the control's container, then the container's window, and eventually up to the application itself. The first object that can handle the event correctly should grab it and stop the event from further bubbling.

In other words, if you want to process your notifications using a hierarchical chain of objects, this is your pattern.

Here's an example which implements a help interface in a layered application. Say the user right-clicks an element in the UI and requests help for a particular visual element. If the front end of the application can handle the help request, it will handle that request; if it can't, it passes that request on to the intermediate layer of the application; if the help request still can't be handled, it's passed on to the application object itself, which displays a default message.

Creating a help interface

To keep control over the objects in your chain, make them all implement the same interface. In this example, I use an interface named `Help`, with one method, `getHelp`, which is passed an `int` constant that describes which help message is required.

```
interface HelpInterface
{
  public void getHelp(int helpConstant);
}
```

Creating chainable objects

There are three application layers that can deal with a help request in this example — the front end, the intermediate layer, and the application object — and you want to chain those objects together as shown in Figure 4-8.

Figure 4-8:
Chaining
objects
together.

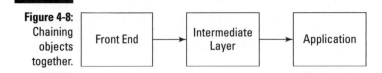

To chain them, you can pass to each object's constructor the next object in the chain — its successor in the chain — as shown here with the FrontEnd class:

```
public class FrontEnd implements HelpInterface
{
  HelpInterface successor;

  public FrontEnd(HelpInterface s)
  {
    successor = s;
  }
      .
      .
      .
  }
}
```

The front end can only handle help requests about the front end, for which I use the constant FRONT_END_HELP. If the constant passed to the FrontEnd object's getHelp method is not FRONT_END_HELP, it should pass the help request to the next object in the chain; otherwise, it knows it can handle this help request and will display a help message as you can see in the following code:

```
public class FrontEnd implements HelpInterface
{
  final int FRONT_END_HELP = 1;
  HelpInterface successor;

  public FrontEnd(HelpInterface s)
  {
    successor = s;
  }

  public void getHelp(int helpConstant)
  {
    if(helpConstant != FRONT_END_HELP){
      successor.getHelp(helpConstant);
    } else {
      System.out.println("This is the front end. Don't you like it?");
    }
  }
}
```

The intermediate layer, class `IntermediateLayer`, can handle help requests corresponding to the `INTERMEDIATE_LAYER_HELP` constant. If it gets passed that constant in the `getHelp` method, it displays a help message — otherwise, it passes the help request on to the next object in the chain.

```
public class IntermediateLayer implements HelpInterface
{
  final int INTERMEDIATE_LAYER_HELP = 2;
  HelpInterface successor;

  public IntermediateLayer(HelpInterface s)
  {
    successor = s;
  }

  public void getHelp(int helpConstant)
  {
    if(helpConstant != INTERMEDIATE_LAYER_HELP){
      successor.getHelp(helpConstant);
    } else {
      System.out.println("This is the intermediate layer. Nice, eh?");
    }
  }
}
```

The end of the chain is the `Application` object; the buck stops here. There is no successor to this link in the chain, so if the `getHelp` method is called in the `Application` object, it just displays a default message.

```
public class Application implements HelpInterface
{

  public Application()
  {
  }

  public void getHelp(int helpConstant)
  {
    System.out.println("This is the MegaGigaCo application.");
  }
}
```

That gives you all the links in the chain. And it's a simple matter to connect them all.

Testing the Help system

You can test all this out in a test harness named `TestHelp.java`. This file creates an `Application`, `FrontEnd`, and `IntermediateLayer` object, and you chain them together by passing the successor to each object to the object's constructor. When the chain is complete, the code calls the front end's `getHelp` method with a constant named `GENERAL_HELP`.

```
public class TestHelp
{
  public static void main(String args[])
  {
    final int FRONT_END_HELP = 1;
    final int INTERMEDIATE_LAYER_HELP = 2;
    final int GENERAL_HELP = 3;

    Application app = new Application();

    IntermediateLayer intermediateLayer = new IntermediateLayer(app);

    FrontEnd frontEnd = new FrontEnd(intermediateLayer);

    frontEnd.getHelp(GENERAL_HELP);
  }
}
```

Since the front end can't handle help requests of this kind, it passes the request on to the intermediate layer. Since that layer can't handle the help request either, the request is passed on to the application object. And the application object displays its generic message:

```
This is the MegaGigaCo application.
```

There you have it; the Chain of Responsibility design pattern at work. Want to handle notifications in a loosely coupled way, but also have a definite chain of command in mind? This is the pattern for you.

Chapter 5

From One to Many: The Singleton and Flyweight Patterns

In your capacity as highly paid consultant to MegaGigaCo, you're troubleshooting some performance issues. "Everything just goes really slowly," say the company programmers.

"Hmm," you say, "I notice you have a really big database object, about 20 megabytes."

"Yep," they say.

"How many of these objects do you have at any one time?"

"About 219," the company programmers say.

"So you have 219 20-megabyte objects when your code is running?" you ask. "Does anyone see a problem with that?"

"Nope," they say.

You tell them, "You're using too many system resources. You've got hundreds of huge objects that you're expecting the computer to handle. Do you really need all those objects?"

"Well. . . . ," they say.

"I thought not," you say. "I'll fix your problem using the Singleton design pattern. For a few megabucks."

"Hmm," they say, "now it's you that's straining the system resources."

This chapter is about taking control of the number of objects you have floating around in your code. There are two patterns especially helpful here: the Singleton design pattern and the Flyweight design pattern.

With the Singleton design pattern, you have only one object of a particular class throughout your code. With the Flyweight pattern, you might also have only one object of a particular class — but it looks to your code as though it's many different objects. A neat trick.

Instantiating Just One Object with the Singleton Pattern

I start with the Singleton pattern and tackle the MegaGigaCo programmers' problem: They want to make sure they create only one object of a particular class, no matter how hard other people's code tries to create multiple objects.

The company programmers are creating hundreds of Database objects in their code, and that's a problem because each object is huge. What's the solution? The Singleton pattern to the rescue.

The Singleton design pattern is all about making sure that you can instantiate only one object of a particular class. If you don't use a pattern like this one, the new operator just keeps on creating more and more objects — each a separate, new object — of the same class as shown in Figure 5-1:

Figure 5-1:
Creating
object1,
object2,
object3, and
many more.

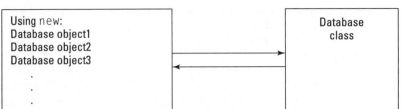

To make sure you only have one object, no matter how many times someone's code tries to create more objects, use the Singleton design pattern. The Gang of Four (GoF) book (*Design Patterns: Elements of Reusable Object-Oriented Software,* 1995, Pearson Education, Inc. Publishing as Pearson Addison Wesley) says that the Singleton design pattern must: "Ensure a class only has one instance, and provide a global point of access to it."

You use the Singleton design pattern when you want to either restrict resource use (instead of creating numbers of large objects without limit) or when you have a sensitive object whose data shouldn't be accessed by multiple instances (such as a registry).

Besides registry objects, you can use the Singleton pattern when you want to restrict the number of objects created because you want to *share* the data in those objects — as when you have a window object or dialog object that displays and modifies data, and you don't want to create multiple objects, which might confuse access to that data.

Creating a single object can also be important when you're multithreading and you don't want conflicts in how the data behind that object is accessed. For example, you may be working with a database object, and if multiple threads each create their own database objects — all of which work with the same underlying data store — you could have a serious issue. I discuss how to work with the Singleton pattern and multithreading in this chapter.

Any time you really want only one object of a certain class, check out the Singleton pattern (instead of the new operator) — it'll get the job done.

The Single and the Fly

The Singleton pattern lets you make sure that no matter how many times your code tries to create an object from a specific class, only one such object is created. That's important in case you've got an object that is so sensitive that conflicts just can't be tolerated, such as an object named, say, windowsRegistry. Using the Singleton pattern lets you take control over the object instantiation process away from the new operator.

The Flyweight pattern is similar to the Singleton pattern. Here, however, the idea is that if your code uses many large objects — using up system resources — you can fix things by using a smaller set of template objects that can be configured on-the-fly to look like those larger objects. The configurable objects — the flyweights — are smaller and reusable (so there are fewer of them), but after being configured, they will appear to the rest of your code as though you still have many large objects.

Creating a Singleton-based database

Time to start slinging some code. Let's say you start with a class named `Database` that the company programmers have been working with. That class has a simple constructor, as shown in the following code:

```
public class Database
{
  private int record;
  private String name;

  public Database(String n)
  {
    name = n;
    record = 0;
  }
        .
        .
        .
}
```

You need to add two built-in methods, `editRecord`, which lets you edit a record in the database, and `getName`, which returns the name of the database.

```
public class Database
{
  private int record;
  private String name;

  public Database(String n)
  {
    name = n;
    record = 0;
  }

  public void editRecord(String operation)
  {
    System.out.println("Performing a " + operation +
      " operation on record " + record +
      " in database " + name);
  }

  public String getName()
  {
    return name;
  }
}
```

Okay so far, but here's the issue: Whenever you use the `new` operator to instantiate an object of the `Database` class, you have to create a new object. Since you have three uses of databases, you have three objects:

```
Database dataOne = new Database("Products");
        .
        .
        .
Database dataTwo = new Database("Products Also");
        .
        .
        .
Database dataThree = new Database("Products Again");
        .
        .
        .
```

How are you going to avoid creating a new object each time someone uses the new operator on your class? Here's one solution — make the constructor *private*.

```
private Database(String n)
{
   name = n;
   record = 0;
}
```

That stops anyone's code from using the new operator, except for the code inside the Database class. But wait a minute — that's crazy, isn't it? Who on Earth would have a private constructor? How could you create objects of such a class if you can't even call the constructor?

Well, some built-in Java classes do it this way. For example, the Graphics and Graphics2D classes both have protected constructors — you can't create an object of these classes directly. Instead, you have to use a utility method, the getGraphics method, to create Graphics or Graphics2D objects. Java does things this way because Graphics objects have to be tailored to the component whose graphics context they support. In other words, you might create a window and then use its getGraphics method to get a Graphics or Graphics2D object. And if you call getGraphics repeatedly, you'll be passed the same Graphics or Graphics2D object.

Sounds good — you give your class a constructor with no public access and let the rest of the world create objects with a utility method that calls that constructor behind the scenes. You can also add code to the utility method to make sure that no more than one object exists.

How would that look in the Database class? First, you make the constructor private:

```
public class Database
{
   private int record;
   private String name;
```

```
private Database(String n)
{
  name = n;
  record = 0;
}
      .
      .
      .
```

Fine, you can block the use of the `new` operator from any code not inside the `Database` class. Now the only way you can create objects of this class is through a utility method, and the usual name for that method when you're using the Singleton pattern is `getInstance` (or `createInstance`, or a more specific name, such as `createDatabase`). Note that this method should be public and also be static so you can call it using just the `Database` class's name (as `Database.getInstance()`).

```
public class Database
{
  private int record;
  private String name;

  private Database(String n)
  {
    name = n;
    record = 0;
  }

  public static Database getInstance(String n)
  {
  }
      .
      .
      .
}
```

This method should return a `Database` object, but that only works when there's one of those in existence. So the code in this method first checks if that object, which I call `singleObject`, exists, and if not, it'll create it. Then it returns that object.

```
public class Database
{
  private static Database singleObject;
  private int record;
  private String name;

  private Database(String n)
  {
```

```
    name = n;
    record = 0;
  }

public static Database getInstance(String n)
  {
      if (singleObject == null){
        singleObject = new Database(n);
      }

      return singleObject;
  }
    .
    .
    .
}
```

Problem solved — now only one object of the Database class exists at one time (although note that there are some multithreading issues coming up, as I discuss in the section "Uh oh — don't forget about multithreading" later in this chapter). Calling the getInstance method gives you a Database object like the one shown in Figure 5-2:

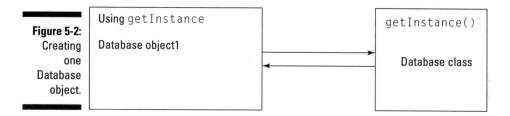

Figure 5-2: Creating one Database object.

When you call getInstance again, you're passed the same object as the first time (see Figure 5-3).

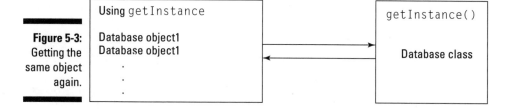

Figure 5-3: Getting the same object again.

No matter how many times you call getInstance, you're passed the same object. Is this going to work as it should? There's one way to find out.

Testing the Singleton pattern

Here's a test harness for the new Singleton `Database` class, `TestSingleton.java`. It starts by getting a `Database` object named `products` using the `Database` class's `getInstance` method and then displays the name of the `Database` object, as stored in that object.

```
public class TestSingleton
{
  public static void main(String args[])
  {
    Database database;

    database = Database.getInstance("products");

    System.out.println("This is the " +
      database.getName() + " database.");
        .
        .
        .
  }
}
```

Then the code gets a `Database` object from the `getInstance` method again, this time passing `employees` as the name to store in the `Database` object.

```
public class TestSingleton
{
  public static void main(String args[])
  {
    Database database;

    database = Database.getInstance("products");

    System.out.println("This is the " +
      database.getName() + " database.");

    database = Database.getInstance("employees");

    System.out.println("This is the " +
      database.getName() + " database.");
  }
}
```

But a `Database` object has already been created, so the second time around, you should still be dealing with the same `Database` object, not a new one. You can check that by looking at the output of this code:

```
This is the products database.
This is the products database.
```

Sure enough, you got the `products` database both times — the `Database` class did what it should: Only one `Database` object was created. There you have it; by restricting access to a class's constructor and allowing objects to be created only with a utility method, you've implemented the Singleton pattern.

Or have you?

Uh oh, don't forget about multithreading

Take a look at the `getInstance` method you've put together in the preceding sections.

```
public static Database getInstance(String n)
{
    if (singleObject == null){
      singleObject = new Database(n);
    }

    return singleObject;
}
```

There's a potential flaw here — a small but definite flaw, which has to do with multithreading. Remember, you want to guarantee that only one `Database` object exists. But when you have multiple threads running through your code, you might have a problem here. In particular, note the test that determines whether or not a `Database` object has already been created:

```
public static Database getInstance(String n)
{
    if (singleObject == null){
      singleObject = new Database(n);
    }

    return singleObject;
}
```

If two threads are making this test at the same time, and no `Database` object exists yet, they could conceivably *both* get past the `if (singleObject == null)` test — which means both threads will create a `Database` object.

How can you fix this? One easy fix is to use the Java `synchronized` keyword, which you can use to restrict access to `getInstance` to one thread at a time. Here's what that looks like:

```
public class DatabaseSynchronized
{
  private static DatabaseSynchronized singleObject;
  private int record;
  private String name;
```

```
private DatabaseSynchronized(String n)
{
  name = n;
  record = 0;
}

public static synchronized DatabaseSynchronized getInstance(String n)
{
    if (singleObject == null){
      singleObject = new DatabaseSynchronized(n);
    }

    return singleObject;
}

public void editRecord(String operation)
{
  System.out.println("Performing a " + operation +
    " operation on record " + record +
    " in database " + name);
}

public String getName()
{
  return name;
}
}
```

Using the synchronized keyword blocks access to the getInstance method
by any new thread once a thread is executing code inside the method; any new
threads attempting to get in have to wait until the current thread is finished.
Using synchronized is one easy way to enforce single-threaded execution,
and in this case, it solves the problem.

Putting the synchronized solution to work

Because access to getInstance is synchronized, you can call it from multiple threads. TestSingletonSynchronized.java puts the synchronized
solution to work. This code starts by calling getInstance to create a
DatabaseSynchronized object, giving it the internal name products.

```
public class TestSingletonSynchronized implements Runable
{
  public static void main(String args[])
  {
    TestSingletonSynchronized t = new TestSingletonSynchronized();
  }

  public TestSingletonSynchronized()
  {
```

```
      DatabaseSynchronized database;

      database = DatabaseSynchronized.getInstance("products");
         .
         .
         .
}
```

The code also launches a new thread to attempt to create a new
DatabaseSynchronized object.

```
public class TestSingletonSynchronized implements Runable
{
  Thread thread;

  public static void main(String args[])
  {
    TestSingletonSynchronized t = new TestSingletonSynchronized();
  }

  public TestSingletonSynchronized()
  {
    DatabaseSynchronized database;

    database = DatabaseSynchronized.getInstance("products");

    thread = new Thread(this, "second");
    thread.start();

    System.out.println("This is the " +
      database.getName() + " database.");
  }
      .
      .
      .
}
```

The new thread's code tries to create a DatabaseSynchronized object with
the internal name employees.

```
public class TestSingletonSynchronized implements Runable
{
  Thread thread;

  public static void main(String args[])
  {
    TestSingletonSynchronized t = new TestSingletonSynchronized();
  }

  public TestSingletonSynchronized()
  {
    DatabaseSynchronized database;
```

```
    database = DatabaseSynchronized.getInstance("products");

    thread = new Thread(this, "second");
    thread.start();

    System.out.println("This is the " +
      database.getName() + " database.");
  }

  public void run()
  {
    DatabaseSynchronized database =
      DatabaseSynchronized.getInstance("employees");

    System.out.println("This is the " +
      database.getName() + " database.");
  }
}
```

But as you can see when you run this code, only one `DatabaseSynchronized` object exists — the originally created `products` database.

```
This is the products database.
This is the products database.
```

As soon as you synchronize the `getInstance` method, you don't have to worry about it anymore — only one thread can be in that method executing code at a time. That locks the object-creation code behind safe walls, which means that it'll do its thing as it should — test to see if the object it's supposed to create already exists, and if not, create it.

At first glance, this appears to be excellent; synchronizing the `getInstance` method solves the multithreading issue and protects the code against conflict conditions where multiple objects could be created by mistake.

However, there's still a question — synchronizing the code works, but is it the best way to accomplish the task? Synchronizing code involves a lot of overhead code that Java adds to monitor what's going on with threads. And it slows your code down significantly, for two reasons: The entrance to the synchronized method has to be constantly monitored, especially when a thread is inside the method executing code, and because synchronized code blocks threads to avoid conflicts, threads end up twiddling their thumbs and losing you time.

Synchronizing `getInstance` works but at a substantial cost. Is there a better way of doing things? You bet.

Handling threading better

The problem you're trying to fix with the `synchronized` keyword is that you don't want the test that checks whether the single object has been created to be corrupted by multiple threads. A better way of doing things is to make sure that test isn't necessary at all.

"How's that?" the company programmers ask in astonishment. "If you're not going to test if the object hasn't already been created, how can you be sure you're not creating a new one?"

You explain, "By stripping all the object-creation code out of the `getInstance` method altogether. I'm going to rewrite the code so that only one object can be created, period. And it'll be created before any thread gets its hands on that object."

"Hmm," say the company programmers. "Sounds like it might work."

Here's the idea — you create the object you want only one of when the code is first loaded into the Java Virtual Machine (the JVM, which is what runs Java code). Don't let `getInstance` create any objects at all — let it return only that one object that's already been created. You can create that single object when the JVM first loads the code like this in `DatabaseThreaded.java`:

```
public class DatabaseThreaded
{
  private static DatabaseThreaded singleObject =
    new DatabaseThreaded("products");
  private int record;
  private String name;

  private DatabaseThreaded(String n)
  {
    name = n;
    record = 0;
  }

        .
        .
        .

}
```

Fine, now you've created the single object you want — there's no reason for any object-creation code in this class. And there's no reason to perform tests to see if the code has already been created. All you have to do is to return the object when the `getInstance` method is called.

```java
public class DatabaseThreaded
{
  private static DatabaseThreaded singleObject =
    new DatabaseThreaded("products");
  private int record;
  private String name;

  private DatabaseThreaded(String n)
  {
    name = n;
    record = 0;
  }

  public static synchronized DatabaseThreaded getInstance(String n)
  {
      return singleObject;
  }

  public void editRecord(String operation)
  {
    System.out.println("Performing a " + operation +
      " operation on record " + record +
      " in database " + name);
  }

  public String getName()
  {
    return name;
  }
}
```

As you can see, this is simplicity itself. The `singleton` object is created before any threads can get at it and returned as needed. Beautiful.

Putting the pre-thread solution to work

Does it work? As with the synchronized solution, you can put this version to work by creating a `DatabaseThreaded` object by calling the `getInstance` method.

```java
public class TestSingletonThreaded implements Runable
{
  public static void main(String args[])
  {
    TestSingletonThreaded t = new TestSingletonThreaded();
  }

  public TestSingletonThreaded()
```

```
{
  DatabaseThreaded database;

  database = DatabaseThreaded.getInstance("products");
      .
      .
      .
}
```

And you can use another thread to try to create a different DatabaseThreaded object.

```
public class TestSingletonThreaded implements Runable
{
  Thread thread;

  public static void main(String args[])
  {
    TestSingletonThreaded t = new TestSingletonThreaded();
  }

  public TestSingletonThreaded()
  {
    DatabaseThreaded database;

    database = DatabaseThreaded.getInstance("products");

    thread = new Thread(this, "second");
    thread.start();

    System.out.println("This is the " +
      database.getName() + " database.");
  }

  public void run()
  {
    DatabaseThreaded database;

    database = DatabaseThreaded.getInstance("employees");

    System.out.println("This is the " +
      database.getName() + " database.");
  }
}
```

When you put all this to work, you see that you're indeed dealing with the same object.

```
This is the products database.
This is the products database.
```

This is a better solution than synchronizing the `getInstance` method — there's no possibility of creating more than one object, so there's not going to be any conflict between threads. You've removed all the overhead involved with synchronizing code just by taking the object-creation code out of the `getInstance` method.

If you're using a version of Java before 1.2 (we're talking early days here), there was a problem with the garbage collector that could spell problems. If there is no reference to the `singleton` object outside the singleton itself, as here, the garbage collector might swallow that object. That bug was fixed in Java 1.2.

Here's something to be careful of — if you're using multiple class loaders and `singleton` objects, you might end up with issues. Because each class loader uses its own namespace, you might in fact end up with multiple `singleton` objects. So if you're using multiple class loaders, make sure your code coordinates among them to ensure only one `singleton` object exists at any one time.

The Flyweight Pattern Makes One Look like Many

The Singleton pattern is all about having a single object, and all your code knows is: you've got only one, single object. There's another pattern that also is all about restricting object creation, but this time it gives the rest of your code the feeling of multiple objects. That's the Flyweight pattern.

This pattern is called *flyweight* because instead of having to work with many massive, individual objects, you whittle them down to a smaller set of more generic objects, called *flyweights,* that can be configured at runtime to look like the more plentiful, massive objects. Each massive object consumes system resources; by extracting what's generic from those massive objects and relying on runtime configuration to mimic those massive objects, you save those resources.

You take all the specialized contents out of the massive objects to create flyweight objects. When you do that, you end up with more-generic objects, and you can reduce the number you need — possibly down to just one — which can be configured as needed at runtime to mimic the larger set of more massive objects.

Alternatives to Singletons

The way of working with singletons I've presented involves handling them as objects, but there is an alternative in Java that bears discussing — simply making all the methods and variables in a class static. That can work, but usually it's best to confine such a way of doing things to simple, self-contained objects. If you start working with multiple classes and anything but the simplest initialization of your objects, you can start running into problems that are very subtle, especially when Java thinks you're mixing static and non-static code. The best way of creating singletons, for most practical, real-world applications, is the way I've presented it here.

As an alternative to static methods and variables, you might also have considered global objects as singletons, and it's true that if you have just one global object of a particular class, that object is shared in the scope in which it's visible. But there are a few things to think about here — starting with one of the primary tenants of OOP (object-oriented programming): encapsulation. That is, it's not good to clutter your namespace. Global objects aren't cool anymore, and haven't been since OOP was brought in to handle large programs. The whole inspiration behind OOP is to remove clutter from namespaces, not the reverse. And the other point is that just because you have only one such global object at a particular time doesn't mean another one can't be created inadvertently in another namespace, giving you some very hard-to-debug issues. The singleton code presented in this section makes sure that only one object can be created; when you work with global variables across different namespaces, there is no such built-in guarantee.

Another issue worth discussing: subclassing a singleton is not a good idea — at best, the constructor will have to be made protected, which means various subclasses can work with it. If you're in a situation where you think you have to start subclassing a singleton, better think twice — is the object you're working with really a singleton? If so, why do you need to subclass it at all?

The GoF book says the Flyweight pattern must, "Use sharing to support large numbers of fine-grained objects efficiently." They go on to say, "A flyweight is a shared object that can be used in multiple contexts simultaneously. The flyweight acts as an independent object in each context — it's indistinguishable from an instance of the object that's not shared."

Here's what happens. Say you start with a large set of massive objects in your code. You remove from those objects all the specialized, instance-specific contents that you can to end up with a shareable object, a flyweight, that acts like a template. That template object can then be configured at runtime by passing it all the specialized contents it needs to appear like one of the more massive objects. So you start with a set of heavy, resource-intensive objects like the ones shown in Figure 5-4.

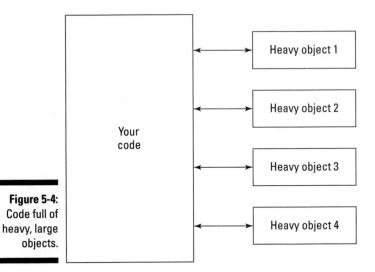

Figure 5-4:
Code full of
heavy, large
objects.

From the heavy objects, you then go to a smaller number of flyweight objects (just one here, but note that the actual number depends on your application) that you configure at runtime to give the appearance of multiple, larger objects (see Figure 5-5).

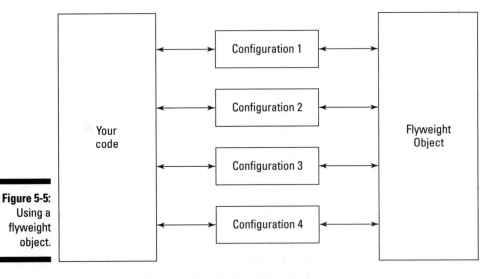

Figure 5-5:
Using a
flyweight
object.

Whenever you've got a large number of massive objects that are putting a strain on your application, the Flyweight pattern should pop into your mind. If you can extract the specialized content from each such object that makes it unique and create a flyweight or set of flyweights that can act as customizable templates, this can be the way to go.

For example, say that in your capacity as a design pattern expert, you've been chosen to teach a class on design patterns. The software you've been given to track student records gives each student his or her own object, and a big one it is, too. You decide that it's time to start saving some system resources. This is a job for the Flyweight pattern.

Creating a student

To simplify the student-tracking code, you decide to have one configurable Flyweight object named Student. This object has to be configurable to look like as many students as needed, so you have to add getter/setter methods to get and set data, such as the student's name, ID, and test score.

You might also want to be able to compare how this student did with respect to the other students, so you add a method called getStanding, which returns the student's offset from average.

Here's what the Student class — the flyweight class in this example — looks like:

```
public class Student
{
  String name;
  int id;
  int score;
  double averageScore;

  public Student(double a)
  {
    averageScore = a;
  }

  public void setName(String n)
  {
    name = n;
  }

  public void setId(int i)
  {
    id = i;
  }

  public void setScore(int s)
  {
    score = s;
  }

  public String getName()
  {
    return name;
```

```
    }

    public int getID()
    {
        return id;
    }

    public int getScore()
    {
        return score;
    }

    public double getStanding()
    {
        return (((double) score) / averageScore - 1.0) * 100.0;
    }
}
```

Note the getStanding method at the very end of this code, which returns the percentage by which the student's score differs from the average score. Okay, now you have a configurable object that you can use to track the progress of each student in the class. It's time to see if it works.

Testing the Flyweight pattern

To use the Flyweight pattern, you've got to keep track of the data you want to use to configure the flyweight to appear like various, more massive objects. In this case, you want to configure a Student object to appear like a set of real students, so you might store the students' data (names, IDs, and test scores) in a set of arrays like this in TestFlyweight.java:

```
public class TestFlyweight
{
    public static void main(String args[])
    {
        String names[] = {"Ralph", "Alice", "Sam"};
        int ids[] = {1001, 1002, 1003};
        int scores[] = {45, 55, 65};
            .
            .
            .
```

To compare a particular student to the other students, you'll also need to determine the average test score, which you find by summing the scores and dividing by the total number of scores:

```
public class TestFlyweight
{
    public static void main(String args[])
    {
```

```
String names[] = {"Ralph", "Alice", "Sam"};
int ids[] = {1001, 1002, 1003};
int scores[] = {45, 55, 65};

double total = 0;
for (int loopIndex = 0; loopIndex < scores.length; loopIndex++){
  total += scores[loopIndex];
}

double averageScore = total / scores.length;
    .
    .
    .
```

In this example, you need only one flyweight Student object, which you create by passing the average test score to the Student constructor:

```
public class TestFlyweight
{
  public static void main(String args[])
  {
    String names[] = {"Ralph", "Alice", "Sam"};
    int ids[] = {1001, 1002, 1003};
    int scores[] = {45, 55, 65};

    double total = 0;
    for (int loopIndex = 0; loopIndex < scores.length; loopIndex++){
      total += scores[loopIndex];
    }

    double averageScore = total / scores.length;

    Student student = new Student(averageScore);
      .
      .
      .
```

Now you can configure the flyweight object as needed, rather than having a dedicated object for each student. Here's what it looks like in a loop that first configures the flyweight object for a particular student, then displays the student's name and standing:

```
public class TestFlyweight
{
  public static void main(String args[])
  {
    String names[] = {"Ralph", "Alice", "Sam"};
    int ids[] = {1001, 1002, 1003};
    int scores[] = {45, 55, 65};

    double total = 0;
    for (int loopIndex = 0; loopIndex < scores.length; loopIndex++){
      total += scores[loopIndex];
```

```
    }

    double averageScore = total / scores.length;

    Student student = new Student(averageScore);

    for (int loopIndex = 0; loopIndex < scores.length; loopIndex++){
      student.setName(names[loopIndex]);
      student.setId(ids[loopIndex]);
      student.setScore(scores[loopIndex]);

      System.out.println("Name: " + student.getName());
      System.out.println("Standing: " +
        Math.round(student.getStanding()));
      System.out.println("");
    }
  }
}
```

Running this code gives you the desired results — the flyweight object is configured for each student on-the-fly, and his or her standing, expressed as a percentage offset from the average score, is displayed.

```
Name: Ralph
Standing: -18

Name: Alice
Standing: 0

Name: Sam
Standing: 18
```

So instead of three full objects, you need only one configurable object. Much like the Singleton pattern, the idea behind the Flyweight pattern is to control object creation and limit the number of objects you need.

Handling threading better

The Flyweight pattern is all about controlling object creation, but you might have noticed that it suffers from the same problem that the Singleton code did earlier in this chapter — if you leave object creation up to the new operator, you might end up with multiple objects when you wanted only a single one, especially if you've got a multithreaded program.

If your code uses multiple threads, you can avoid creating too many flyweight objects by taking the object creation process away from the new operator in the same way you did with singletons. You can create the flyweight object when the class is first loaded, make the constructor private, and allow object creation only through a `getInstance` method:

```
public class StudentThreaded
{
  String name;
  int id;
  int score;
  double averageScore;
  private static StudentThreaded singleObject =
    new StudentThreaded();

  private StudentThreaded()
  {
  }

  public void setAverageScore(double a)
  {
    averageScore = a;
  }

  public void setName(String n)
  {
    name = n;
  }

  public void setId(int i)
  {
    id = i;
  }

  public void setScore(int s)
  {
    score = s;
  }

  public String getName()
  {
    return name;
  }

  public int getID()
  {
    return id;
  }

  public int getScore()
  {
    return score;
  }
```

```
public double getStanding()
{
    return (((double) score) / averageScore - 1.0) * 100.0;
}

public static StudentThreaded getInstance()
{
    return singleObject;
}

}
```

This code, `TestFlyweightThreaded.java`, puts to work this new version of the flyweight by creating a student object and accessing it both from the main thread and a worker thread.

```
public class TestFlyweightThreaded implements Runable
{
  Thread thread;

  public static void main(String args[])
  {
    TestFlyweightThreaded t = new TestFlyweightThreaded();
  }

  public TestFlyweightThreaded()
  {
    String names[] = {"Ralph", "Alice", "Sam"};
    int ids[] = {1001, 1002, 1003};
    int scores[] = {45, 55, 65};

    double total = 0;
    for (int loopIndex = 0; loopIndex < scores.length; loopIndex++){
      total += scores[loopIndex];
    }

    double averageScore = total / scores.length;

    StudentThreaded student = StudentThreaded.getInstance();

    student.setAverageScore(averageScore);
    student.setName("Ralph");
    student.setId(1002);
    student.setScore(45);

    thread = new Thread(this, "second");
    thread.start();

    System.out.println("Name: " + student.getName() +
```

```
      ", Standing: " + Math.round(student.getStanding()));
  }

  public void run()
  {
    StudentThreaded student = StudentThreaded.getInstance();

    System.out.println("Name: " + student.getName() +
      ", Standing: " + Math.round(student.getStanding()));
  }
}
```

Running this code gives you this result, where you're clearly dealing with the same object in both the main and secondary threads:

```
Name: Ralph, Standing: -18
Name: Ralph, Standing: -18
```

Does the Flyweight pattern have any drawbacks? Some. The main issue is that it can take some time to configure a flyweight object, and if you're always swapping configurations, you can lose much of the performance gains you hoped to achieve. Another possible drawback: Because you're extracting a generic template class from your existing objects in order to create flyweight objects, you're adding another layer of programming, which can make maintenance and extension harder.

Part II

Becoming an OOP Master

The 5th Wave   By Rich Tennant

With Object-Oriented Programming, I understand the "encapsulation" and "inheritance" part. It's that darn "cluttermorphism" that stumps me.

In this part . . .

In this part, you get the inside scoop on patterns and object-oriented programming (OOP). Patterns have a great deal to say about OOP and about how to improve your object-oriented experience. Many programmers have knee-jerk ways of working with OOP, which are just plain wrong. The design patterns in this part are there to point you to a better way.

Chapter 6

Fitting Round Pegs into Square Holes with the Adapter and Facade Patterns

· ·

In This Chapter

▶ Using the Adapter pattern

▶ Creating adapters

▶ Adapting Ace objects as Acme objects

▶ Handling adapter issues

▶ Using the Facade pattern

· ·

Sometimes, objects just don't fit together as they should. A class may have changed, or an object turns out to be just too difficult to work with. This chapter comes to the rescue by covering two design patterns: the Adapter pattern and the Facade pattern. The Adapter design pattern lets you adapt what an object or class has to offer so that another object or class can make use of it. The Facade design pattern is similar, in that it changes the look of an object, but the goal here is a little different: You use this design pattern to *simplify* the exposed methods of an object or class, making it easier to work with that object or class.

The Adapter Scenario

"Alright," says the MegaGigaCo team leader, entering the room, "hold everything. Management has decreed that we switch our back-end framework to the one sold by the CEO's nephew's company."

"Hmm," says a programmer, "that could be a problem. Our online user interface takes customer orders using software from the Ace company and packages them in objects of the Ace class. What type of objects can we pass to the new back end?"

"Only the new Acme objects," the team leader says, "not Ace objects."

"Uh oh," everyone says. "There go our jobs."

You can see the problem. Currently, the Ace objects that are passed to the back end fit right in, as shown in Figure 6-1.

Figure 6-1:
These two
objects fit
together
well.

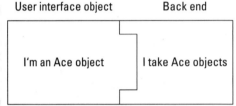

But when the back end is switched to take Acme objects (instead of Ace objects), the current Ace objects created by the user interface won't fit. That scenario looks like Figure 6-2.

Figure 6-2:
The user
interface no
longer
works with
the back
end.

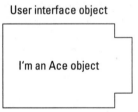
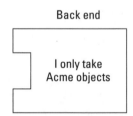

"I have the solution," you say. Everyone turns to you and you say, "Of course, as a consultant, I'll have to charge a whopper fee on this."

"Anything," the team leader says. "The mortgage folks don't understand about missing payments if I lose my job."

"You need to use the Adapter pattern," you explain. "The Adapter pattern lets you adapt what an object or class exposes to what another object or class expects." You draw the solution on the whiteboard like that shown in Figure 6-3.

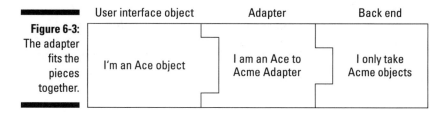

Figure 6-3: The adapter fits the pieces together.

"Ah," says the development team. "We are beginning to understand."

"Fine," you say, "pay me some money."

Fixing Connection Problems with Adapters

The Adapter design pattern lets you fix the interface between objects and classes without having to modify the objects or classes directly. When you're working with store-bought applications, you often can't get inside to alter what one application produces to make it more palatable to another application.

This is particularly important in online development. As more and more companies start going for larger-scale enterprise solutions, they're ditching the smaller corporations' software in favor of soup-to-nuts solutions from the big boys like IBM. And that's a shame because the issue is almost always one of compatibility — the smaller corporation's software can't talk to one or two other components in the whole system. But turning to an expensive solution isn't always necessary. Usually, the problems can be fixed with a small adapter. In other words, letting the big boys win at your expense could be avoided with just a little effort here.

How the Adapter pattern works is best seen in an example. Currently, the MegaGigaCo user interface, which I discuss in previous sections of this chapter, packages user data in objects of the `Ace` class. This class handles customer names with these two methods:

- ✔ setName
- ✔ getName

But, as you know, MegaGigaCo is switching to Acme software for the back end, which has to be able to handle customer orders in a different way. The problem is that the Acme back end expects customer orders to be packaged in `Acme` objects. And `Acme` objects use four methods, not two, to handle the customer's name. They are:

- ✔ `setFirstName`
- ✔ `setLastName`
- ✔ `getFirstName`
- ✔ `getLastName`

So you need an adapter to make sure that the Acme back end can handle `Ace` objects. This adapter calls the two methods supported by the `Ace` object and extends that into a set of four methods that `Acme` objects usually offer, as shown in Figure 6-4.

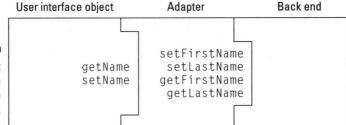

Figure 6-4:
The Ace and Acme adapter.

User interface object	Adapter	Back end
getName setName	setFirstName setLastName getFirstName getLastName	

That's the idea and what the Adapter design pattern is all about.

The Gang of Four (GoF) book (*Design Patterns: Elements of Reusable Object-Oriented Software,* 1995, Pearson Education, Inc. Publishing as Pearson Addison Wesley) says the Adapter pattern lets you "Convert the interface of a class into another interface the client expects. Adapter lets classes work together that couldn't otherwise because of incompatible interfaces."

Although the official definition of the Adapter pattern talks about classes, this pattern actually has two variations: one for objects and one for classes. I look at both in this chapter.

You use the Adapter design pattern when you're trying to fit a square peg into a round hole. If what a class or object exposes isn't what you need to end up with, you can add an adapter — much like an electrical outlet adapter for international travel — to give you what you need.

This design pattern is particularly good when you're working with legacy code that can't be changed, while the software that interacts with that code does change.

Now to get down to actually putting the Adapter pattern to work.

Creating Ace objects

Before the CEO's nephew ruined everything for your department, `Ace` objects handled customer names with just two methods: `setName` and `getName` — here's an interface which specifies those two methods:

```
public interface AceInterface
{
  public void setName(String n);
  public String getName();
}
```

The `Ace` objects that came out of the user interface were objects of the `AceClass`, which implemented this interface:

```
public class AceClass implements AceInterface
{
    .
    .
    .
}
```

The two methods, `setName` and `getName`, were simplicity itself to add.

```
public class AceClass implements AceInterface
{
  String name;

  public void setName(String n)
  {
    name = n;
  }

  public String getName()
  {
    return name;
  }
}
```

That's all you needed when the user interface produced Ace objects and the back end consumed Ace objects. But now the company is switching to an Acme back end, which consumes Acme objects. (Thanks again to that nephew!)

Creating Acme objects

Acme objects must handle customer names with four methods: setFirst Name, setLastName, getFirstName, and getLastName. Here's an interface, AcmeInterface, which lists these methods:

```
public interface AcmeInterface
{
   public void setFirstName(String f);
   public void setLastName(String l);
   public String getFirstName();
   public String getLastName();
}
```

Acme objects are based on the Acme class, which implements the AcmeInterface.

```
public class AcmeClass implements AcmeInterface
{
     .
     .
     .
}
```

Here are the four methods this class exposes:

```
public class AcmeClass implements AcmeInterface
{
   String firstName;
   String lastName;

   public void setFirstName(String f)
   {
     firstName = f;
   }

   public void setLastName(String l)
   {
     lastName = l;
   }

   public String getFirstName()
   {
```

```
    return firstName;
  }

  public String getLastName()
  {
    return lastName;
  }
}
```

At this point, you've got the `Ace` objects produced by the user interface and the `Acme` objects consumed by the back end. Now you've got to create an adapter that lets you plug `Ace` objects into the Acme back end.

Creating an Ace-to-Acme object adapter

You want to create an adapter to let software that expects an `Acme` object to actually work with an `Ace` object, so you should create an object adapter. Object adapters work by *composition* (see Chapter 2 for more on composition) — the adapter stores the object it's adapting inside itself.

Continuing with the example in this chapter, I name the adapter `AceToAcme Adapter`, and because it has to look like an `Acme` object, it implements the `AcmeInterface` interface.

```
public class AceToAcmeAdapter implements AcmeInterface
{
    .
    .
    .
}
```

This adapter uses object composition to hold the object it's supposed to be adapting, an `AceClass` object. You can pass that object to the adapter's constructor, which will store the `Ace` object.

```
public class AceToAcmeAdapter implements AcmeInterface
{
  AceClass aceObject;

  public AceToAcmeAdapter(AceClass a)
  {
    aceObject = a;
  }
    .
    .
    .
}
```

The difference between `Ace` and `Acme` objects is that `Ace` objects store the customer's name as a single string, while `Acme` objects store the first name and last name separately. To adapt between `Ace` and `Acme` objects, I split the name stored in the `Ace` object passed to the constructor into first and last names. You can recover the customer name from the stored `Ace` object using its `getName` method.

```java
public class AceToAcmeAdapter implements AcmeInterface
{
  AceClass aceObject;
  String firstName;
  String lastName;

  public AceToAcmeAdapter(AceClass a)
  {
    aceObject = a;
    firstName = aceObject.getName().split(" ")[0];
    lastName = aceObject.getName().split(" ")[1];
  }
}
```

Now you've got the customer's first and last names. To mimic an `Acme` object, you have to implement the `Acme` methods `setFirstName`, `setLastName`, `getFirstName`, and `getLastName`, returning or setting the customer's first and last names as needed. Here's what those methods look like:

```java
public class AceToAcmeAdapter implements AcmeInterface
{
  AceClass aceObject;
  String firstName;
  String lastName;

  public AceToAcmeAdapter(AceClass a)
  {
    aceObject = a;
    firstName = aceObject.getName().split(" ")[0];
    lastName = aceObject.getName().split(" ")[1];
  }

  public void setFirstName(String f)
  {
    firstName = f;
  }

  public void setLastName(String l)
  {
    lastName = l;
  }

  public String getFirstName()
```

```
  {
    return firstName;
  }

  public String getLastName()
  {
    return lastName;
  }
}
```

Excellent — you've got your adapter. Is it going to work?

Testing the adapter

Throughout this section, you have been adapting `Ace` objects so they look like `Acme` objects. Now it's time to see if the Adapter pattern is working the way you want it to. You can test this with the `TestAdapter.java` test harness, which starts by creating an `Ace` object that contains the customer name Cary Grant.

```
public class TestAdapter
{
  public static void main(String args[])
  {
    AceClass aceObject = new AceClass();

    aceObject.setName("Cary Grant");
      .
      .
      .
  }
}
```

Then you pass this `Ace` object to an `AceToAcmeAdapter` object.

```
public class TestAdapter
{
  public static void main(String args[])
  {
    AceClass aceObject = new AceClass();

    aceObject.setName("Cary Grant");

    AceToAcmeAdapter adapter = new AceToAcmeAdapter(aceObject);
      .
      .
      .
  }
}
```

And you're good to go — you can use the Acme methods like getFirstName and getLastName with no problem.

```
public class TestAdapter
{
  public static void main(String args[])
  {
    AceClass aceObject = new AceClass();

    aceObject.setName("Cary Grant");

    AceToAcmeAdapter adapter = new AceToAcmeAdapter(aceObject);

    System.out.println("Customer's first name: " +
      adapter.getFirstName());
    System.out.println("Customer's last name: " +
      adapter.getLastName());
  }
}
```

Running this code gives you:

```
Customer's first name: Cary
Customer's last name: Grant
```

Just what you'd expect if you were using a bona fide Acme object; the calling code need never know it's not dealing with an Acme object.

That's how object adapters work. An adapter uses composition to store the object it's supposed to adapt, and when the adapter's methods are called, it translates those calls into something the adapted object can understand and passes the calls on to the adapted object. The code that calls the adapter never needs to know that it's not dealing with the kind of object it thinks it is, but an adapted object instead.

Using object composition to wrap the adapted object is good object-oriented design, as discussed in Chapter 2. And note that if you subclass the adapted object, the adapter wrapper will be able to handle the subclassed objects with minimal changes.

Inheriting class adapters

There's another kind of adapter besides object adapters — class adapters. You explain to the company programmers: "While object adapters use composition to store the object they're adapting, class adapters are designed to use multiple inheritance to merge the adapted class and the class you're adapting it to."

"There's a flaw here," say the company programmers, "if you're working with Java."

"And that is?" you ask.

"Java doesn't support multiple inheritance," they say.

"Right you are," you say. "Which means you can't create true class adapters in Java."

The GoF book uses languages like C++ and Smalltalk when discussing class adapters, but not Java because Java doesn't support multiple inheritance. If it did, you could inherit from both the adapted class and the target class you want to mimic in an adapter class, as you can see in Figure 6-5.

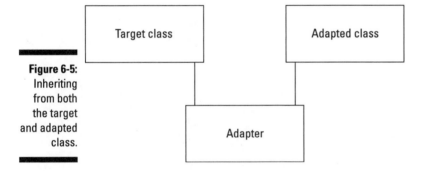

Figure 6-5:
Inheriting
from both
the target
and adapted
class.

Here's an example using single inheritance in Java, which is as close as you can get to creating class adapters. The user interface team comes to you and says, "We like Java AWT check boxes, and we're not so fond of Swing check boxes."

"Ever thought of entering the 21st century?" you ask.

Ignoring the cheap jab, the UI (user interface) team says, "The problem is that the rest of the user interface uses Swing — and we want to not only stick with AWT check boxes, but also make them look like Swing check boxes to any Swing code that needs to use them."

"That's going to be expensive," you say.

"Do we need to put in a special request to Sun Microsystems?" they ask.

"No, I'll do it. But it's going to cost you plenty."

You write the user interface code for Swing check boxes and determine if a check box is checked using the isSelected method. But AWT check boxes don't support isSelected; the AWT method is getState. So you need an adapter to wrap an SWT check box and adapt the getState to isSelected instead, as shown in Figure 6-6.

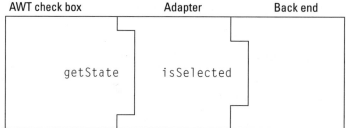

AWT check box   Adapter   Back end

getState   isSelected

Figure 6-6:
Using an
adapter
between
AWT and
SWT.

The class adapter, CheckboxAdapter, is going to inherit from the AWT Checkbox class.

```
import java.awt.*;

public class CheckboxAdapter extends Checkbox
{
        .
        .
        .
}
```

The public constructor passes control back to the AWT Checkbox constructor this way:

```
import java.awt.*;

public class CheckboxAdapter extends Checkbox
{
    public CheckboxAdapter(String n)
    {
      super(n);
    }
        .
        .
        .
}
```

To implement the isSelected method of the CheckboxAdapter class, you just pass on the data you get back from the AWT getState method.

```
import java.awt.*;

public class CheckboxAdapter extends Checkbox
{
    public CheckboxAdapter(String n)
    {
      super(n);
    }

    public boolean isSelected()
    {
      return getState();
    }
}
```

You can use the adapted check boxes in Swing UI code; here's how that works in an example, Checkboxes.java, which builds a JFrame object that implements the ItemListener interface to catch check box events:

```
import java.awt.*;
import javax.swing.*;
import java.awt.event.*;

public class Checkboxes extends JFrame implements ItemListener
{
}
```

The main method creates a new Checkboxes object and displays it.

```
import java.awt.*;
import javax.swing.*;
import java.awt.event.*;

public class Checkboxes extends JFrame implements ItemListener
{
        .
        .
        .
    public static void main(String args[])
    {
        final Checkboxes f = new Checkboxes();

        f.setBounds(100, 100, 400, 300);
        f.setVisible(true);
        f.setDefaultCloseOperation(DISPOSE_ON_CLOSE);

        f.addWindowListener(new WindowAdapter() {
            public void windowClosing(WindowEvent e) {
                System.exit(0);
            }
        });
    }
}
```

The Checkboxes constructor creates four CheckboxAdapter objects and adds them to the content pane.

```java
import java.awt.*;
import javax.swing.*;
import java.awt.event.*;

public class Checkboxes extends JFrame implements ItemListener
{
    CheckboxAdapter checks[];
    JTextField text;

    public Checkboxes()
    {
        Container contentPane = getContentPane();
        contentPane.setLayout(new FlowLayout());

        checks = new CheckboxAdapter[4];

        for(int loopIndex = 0; loopIndex
          <= checks.length - 1; loopIndex++){
            checks[loopIndex] = new CheckboxAdapter("Check " +
              loopIndex);
            checks[loopIndex].addItemListener(this);
            contentPane.add(checks[loopIndex]);
        }

        text = new JTextField(30);

        contentPane.add(text);
    }
        .
        .
        .

    public static void main(String args[])
    {
        final Checkboxes c = new Checkboxes();

        c.setBounds(100, 100, 400, 300);
        c.setVisible(true);
        c.setDefaultCloseOperation(DISPOSE_ON_CLOSE);

        c.addWindowListener(new WindowAdapter() {
            public void windowClosing(WindowEvent e) {
                System.exit(0);
            }
        });
    }
}
```

You can handle the `CheckboxAdapter` objects as you would standard Swing check boxes when it comes to the `isSelected` method. When there's a check box event, the `itemChanged` method will be called, and you can check which of the check boxes is/are checked using `isSelected` in that method — the selected check boxes will be displayed in the text control.

```java
import java.awt.*;
import javax.swing.*;
import java.awt.event.*;

public class Checkboxes extends JFrame implements ItemListener
{
    CheckboxAdapter checks[];
    JTextField text;

    public Checkboxes()
    {
        Container contentPane = getContentPane();
        contentPane.setLayout(new FlowLayout());

        checks = new CheckboxAdapter[4];

        for(int loopIndex = 0; loopIndex
          <= checks.length - 1; loopIndex++){
            checks[loopIndex] = new CheckboxAdapter("Check " +
              loopIndex);
            checks[loopIndex].addItemListener(this);
            contentPane.add(checks[loopIndex]);
        }

        text = new JTextField(30);

        contentPane.add(text);
    }

    public void itemStateChanged(ItemEvent e)
    {
        String outString = new String("Selected: ");

        for(int loopIndex = 0; loopIndex
          <= checks.length - 1; loopIndex++){
            if(checks[loopIndex].isSelected()) {
                outString += " checkbox " + loopIndex;
            }
        }
        text.setText(outString);
    }

    public static void main(String args[])
```

```
    {
        final Checkboxes f = new Checkboxes();

        f.setBounds(100, 100, 400, 300);
        f.setVisible(true);
        f.setDefaultCloseOperation(DISPOSE_ON_CLOSE);

        f.addWindowListener(new WindowAdapter() {
            public void windowClosing(WindowEvent e) {
                System.exit(0);
            }
        });
    }

}
```

So object adapters rely on object composition, while class adapters rely on inheritance. Object adapters can be more flexible because they can work with not just the objects they've been designed to adapt but also subclassed objects of the adapted objects. But with class adapters, you have to modify the class adapter to do the same thing. To be more flexible, in general, don't forget the design principle that says you should favor composition over inheritance.

One final note on adapters — besides adapting the behavior of a class or object, adapters can also *improve* that behavior by adding their own methods. For example, an adapted object that reports temperatures in Fahrenheit might be improved if its adapter also adds a method that reports temperatures in Centigrade.

Drawbacks of adapters? Not many — mostly that there's an additional layer of code added, and so to maintain. But if rewriting legacy code isn't an option, adapters provide a good option.

Simplifying Life with Facades

Similar to the Adapter pattern is the Facade design pattern. These two patterns work in much the same way, but they have different purposes. The Adapter pattern adapts code to work with other code. But the Facade pattern gives you a wrapper that makes the original code easier to deal with.

For example, say that someone's designed a printer and shows it to you proudly. "How do I make it print?" you ask.

"First," he tells you, "call the initialize method."

"Okay," you say. "Now it prints?"

"No, you have to call the `turnFanOn` method."

"Okay. Now it'll print?" you ask.

"Nope. Call the `warmUp` method."

"Alright. Now it prints, right?"

"Not yet. You have to call the `getData` method to get the data from the computer to print."

"Okay, the `getData` method. And next?"

"The `formatData` method."

"And?"

"The `checkToner` method, the `checkPaperSupply` method, the `runInternalDiagnostics` method, the `checkPaperPath` method, the . . . ."

"Hold on," you say, writing a facade for the whole mess. Your facade calls all those methods behind the scenes and dramatically simplifies the interface. "Here you go."

"What's this?" the printer designer asks.

"The `print` method," you say. "Just call the `print` method, and the printer prints. No more to do."

"Hey," he says, "that might be a good idea. Now I can add a `prepareToCallThePrintMethod` method, a `callThePrintMethod` method, a `cleanupAfterPrinting` method, a. . . ."

"You're hopeless," you say.

The Facade design pattern makes an OOP interface (and that's the general use of the term, not just a Java interface) easier to use. It's fundamentally a design issue — if an object or class interface is too hard to work with, the Facade pattern gives you a front end to that interface to make it easier. Here's the official GoF word on the Facade pattern — note that they're also using the term "interface" generically here:

The GoF book says the Facade pattern should "Provide a unified interface to a set of interfaces in a system. Facade defines a higher-level interface that makes the subsystem easier to use."

Often, you use the Facade pattern when you're dealing with poorly encapsulated code. Not everyone is an OOP genius, as you quickly learn when you work in any large-scale commercial software development environment. When you get tired of dealing with an awkwardly-designed interface and find yourself just wishing it did x, y, and/or z simply, that's when it's time for a new interface.

The idea is simple; a facade just simplifies the interface (using the generic sense of the word "interface" here, not a Java interface) between a class or object and the code that makes use of that class or object. (See Figure 6-7.)

Figure 6-7:
The Facade pattern makes an interface less complicated.

I've got a difficult interface	I am the Facade	I only need to deal with a simple interface

You usually use the Facade design pattern when you can't rewrite the code you wish were simpler. Although using a Facade can fix the problem, it adds another layer, and if the underlying code changes, you're going to have to change your Facade pattern as well.

There's an OOP design principle at work here, sometimes called the *Principle of Least Knowledge,* sometimes called the *Law of Demeter,* sometimes just called *effective encapsulation.* The idea is that for effective OOP, you don't want to insist that separate entities (classes of objects) have to know too much about each other. As much as possible, you should lock away the details inside each class or object and make the coupling between entities as loose as possible (see Chapter 4 for more on loose coupling). If one object needs to know too much about another to make their coupling loose, a Facade pattern can help.

Always go for the loosest coupling you can.

Dealing with a difficult object

Here's an example showing how the Facade design pattern can save the day. Your company has just purchased the rival company, and management is jubilant.

"Hmm," you ask, "isn't this going to cause some software incompatibilities? Their product is very different from ours."

"Nonsense," says the Big Boss. "Things couldn't be simpler."

"Well," you ask, "how do you set the name of an object?"

"Couldn't be simpler. Just call the `setFirstNameCharacter` method. That sets the first character of the name."

"Uh, what about the second character of the name?"

"Just call the `setSecondNameCharacter` method. Couldn't be simpler."

"So let me get this straight," you say. "To set the name of an object, you call the `setFirstNameCharacter` method to set the first character of the name, the `setSecondNameCharacter` method to set the second character of the name, all the way up to the `setFiveMillionthNameCharacter` to set the five millionth name character?"

"Nope," says the Big Boss, "you can only set seven-name characters."

"Ah," you say. "Couldn't be simpler."

"Right," says the Big Boss.

Here's the code given to you after the merger to handle the creation of the former rival company's product, `DifficultProduct`.

```
public class DifficultProduct
{
  public DifficultProduct()
  {
  }
  .
  .
  .
}
```

You set the name of this product character by character, using the `setFirst NameCharacter`, `setSecondNameCharacter`, `setThirdNameCharacter`, and so-forth methods, which are already built into this class:

```
public class DifficultProduct
{
  char nameChars[] = new char[7];

  public DifficultProduct()
  {
  }

  public void setFirstNameCharacter(char c)
  {
    nameChars[0] = c;
  }

  public void setSecondNameCharacter(char c)
  {
    nameChars[1] = c;
  }

  public void setThirdNameCharacter(char c)
  {
    nameChars[2] = c;
  }

  public void setFourthNameCharacter(char c)
  {
    nameChars[3] = c;
  }

  public void setFifthNameCharacter(char c)
  {
    nameChars[4] = c;
  }

  public void setSixthNameCharacter(char c)
  {
    nameChars[5] = c;
  }

  public void setSeventhNameCharacter(char c)
  {
    nameChars[6] = c;
  }
  .
  .
  .
}
```

To recover the name of the object, you call the `getName` method, which, sensibly, returns a `String`.

```java
public class DifficultProduct
{
  char nameChars[] = new char[7];

  public DifficultProduct()
  {
  }

  public void setFirstNameCharacter(char c)
  {
    nameChars[0] = c;
  }

  public void setSecondNameCharacter(char c)
  {
    nameChars[1] = c;
  }

  public void setThirdNameCharacter(char c)
  {
    nameChars[2] = c;
  }

  public void setFourthNameCharacter(char c)
  {
    nameChars[3] = c;
  }

  public void setFifthNameCharacter(char c)
  {
    nameChars[4] = c;
  }

  public void setSixthNameCharacter(char c)
  {
    nameChars[5] = c;
  }

  public void setSeventhNameCharacter(char c)
  {
    nameChars[6] = c;
  }

  public String getName()
  {
    return new String(nameChars);
  }
}
```

To set the name of a `DifficultProduct` object, you've got to work letter by letter — here's how you'd create a printer, for example:

```
DifficultProduct difficultProduct = new DifficultProduct();

difficultProduct.setFirstNameCharacter('p');
difficultProduct.setSecondNameCharacter('r');
difficultProduct.setThirdNameCharacter('i');
difficultProduct.setFourthNameCharacter('n');
difficultProduct.setFifthNameCharacter('t');
difficultProduct.setSixthNameCharacter('e');
difficultProduct.setSeventhNameCharacter('r');
```

"See?" asks the Big Boss, "couldn't be easier."

"Enough of this nonsense," you say; "I'm going to write a facade."

Creating a simplifying facade

Your boss has given you your directive, and you get to work on a facade, the `SimpleProductFacade` class, which should look like the following:

```
public class SimpleProductFacade
{
  public SimpleProductFacade()
  {
  }
    .
    .
    .
}
```

This facade is going to wrap the object (`DifficultProduct` in this example). Usually, the way you write a facade is to have the facade modify the object's external interface. You can also pass configuration parameters to the facade's constructor, but that's not needed in this example, which just creates the new `DifficultProduct` object and stores it.

```
public class SimpleProductFacade
{
  DifficultProduct difficultProduct;

  public SimpleProductFacade()
  {
    difficultProduct = new DifficultProduct();
  }
    .
    .
    .
}
```

The problem with the original DifficultObject class is the way you set the object's name, using the clumsy methods setFirstNameCharacter, setSecondNameCharacter, setThirdNameCharacter, and so on. To fix that, you decide to provide the facade with a simple setName method that you pass the name of the object as a string to. That method simply breaks the name from a string to an array of chars, and passes those chars on to the wrapped DifficultObject methods setFirstNameCharacter, setSecondNameCharacter, setThirdNameCharacter, and so on methods:

```java
public class SimpleProductFacade
{
  DifficultProduct difficultProduct;

  public SimpleProductFacade()
  {
    difficultProduct = new DifficultProduct();
  }

  public void setName(String n)
  {
    char chars[] = n.toCharArray();

    if(chars.length > 0){
      difficultProduct.setFirstNameCharacter(chars[0]);
    }

    if(chars.length > 1){
      difficultProduct.setSecondNameCharacter(chars[1]);
    }

    if(chars.length > 2){
      difficultProduct.setThirdNameCharacter(chars[2]);
    }

    if(chars.length > 3){
      difficultProduct.setFourthNameCharacter(chars[3]);
    }

    if(chars.length > 4){
      difficultProduct.setFifthNameCharacter(chars[4]);
    }

    if(chars.length > 5){
      difficultProduct.setSixthNameCharacter(chars[5]);
    }

    if(chars.length > 6){
```

```
      difficultProduct.setSeventhNameCharacter(chars[6]);
   }
}
   .
   .
   .
}
```

Methods that don't need a facade, like the simple getName method, can be passed on to the underlying object without modification.

```
public class SimpleProductFacade
{
  DifficultProduct difficultProduct;

  public SimpleProductFacade()
  {
    difficultProduct = new DifficultProduct();
  }

  public void setName(String n)
  {
    char chars[] = n.toCharArray();

    if(chars.length > 0){
      difficultProduct.setFirstNameCharacter(chars[0]);
    }
      .
      .
      .
    if(chars.length > 6){
      difficultProduct.setSeventhNameCharacter(chars[6]);
    }
  }

  public String getName()
  {
    return difficultProduct.getName();
  }
}
```

Now you've wrapped the difficult object in a facade and exposed a set of simple-to-use methods, setName and getName. The next step is to get it all to actually do something.

Testing the facade

To make sure the facade code does what you want, test it with `TestFacade.java`. This code creates a new `SimpleProductFacade` object, then sets the object's name (`"printer"`) with `setName` and retrieves it with `getName`.

```
public class TestFacade
{
  public static void main(String args[])
  {
    TestFacade t = new TestFacade();
  }

  public TestFacade()
  {
    SimpleProductFacade simpleProductFacade =
      new SimpleProductFacade();

    simpleProductFacade.setName("printer");

    System.out.println("This product is a " +
      simpleProductFacade.getName());
  }
}
```

And you get this, showing you were able to use the new `setName` method to set the name of the object:

```
This product is a printer
```

You've conquered the difficult object and its awkward interface with a facade.

Any facades that already exist in Java? There aren't many built-in examples of facades in Java; Sun's not about to admit that some Java subsection is hard enough to deal with that it has to include a facade to fix things. About the closest you come to facades in Java are, paradoxically, the so-called Adapter classes.

Java Adapter classes make implementing Java interfaces easier because they implement the interface's methods themselves, using empty methods, which means you don't have to. So if you've got a built-in Java interface you want to implement, you can often just use an Adapter class instead and override only those methods you want to change.

The name *adapter* seems to suggest that Java adapters are all about the Adapter design pattern, but remember that the idea behind the Adapter pattern is, as the GoF say, "Adapter lets classes work together that couldn't otherwise because of incompatible interfaces." The Java Adapter classes are more about making an interface easier to work with, which is closer to how the GoF describe the Facade design pattern: "Facade defines a higher-level interface that makes the subsystem easier to use."

Here's an example that puts the Java WindowAdapter to work to handle just the window closing event in an inner class. (If you implemented the WindowListener interface, you'd have seven methods to implement, from windowActivated to windowOpened.)

```java
import java.awt.*;
import java.awt.event.*;

class AppFrame extends Frame
{
    public void paint(Graphics g)
    {
        g.drawString("Using a window adapter", 60, 100);
    }
}

public class app
{
    public static void main(String [] args)
    {
        AppFrame a = new AppFrame();

        a.setSize(200, 200);

        a.addWindowListener(new WindowAdapter() {public void
            windowClosing(WindowEvent e) {System.exit(0);}});

        a.show();
    }
}
```

If you click this window's Close button, the window closes and the application exits, thanks to the WindowAdapter.

Chapter 7

Mass Producing Objects with the Template Method and Builder Patterns

· ·

In This Chapter

▶ Using the Template Method design pattern

▶ Creating robots using template methods

▶ Subclassing template methods

▶ Understanding how the Builder pattern differs from the Template Method pattern

▶ Using the Builder design pattern

· ·

"**G**ood news," says the CEO of GigundoCorp — the new company you're doing consulting work for — while running into the break room. "We landed that contract!"

"What contract?" everyone asks.

"That contract where we build robots that build cars," says the CEO.

"Oh, that contract," everyone says.

"Now get out there and do the software," says the CEO, shooing programmers out the door.

"Just a second," you say. "Shouldn't we take some time to look at the design issues? For example, is it possible you might be building other types of robots in the future?"

"Sure," says the CEO, "we have other bids out there. But there's no time to think about that! We need to get started on those automotive robots!"

"Yeah!" all the programmers cry, running back to their cubicles.

"Something tells me they're going to be sorry," you say to the empty break room, littered with empty Styrofoam cups rolling across the floor.

This chapter is all about two patterns that give you clever ways of dealing with and adapting the process of creating objects: the Template Method pattern, and the Builder pattern. The Template Method pattern lets subclasses redefine the steps involved in creating an object, which is going to be useful here when it's time to create different kinds of robots. And the Builder pattern gives you even more flexibility with the creation process by separating the construction process out into its own object. Both are coming up in this chapter.

Creating the First Robot

The GigundoCorp programmers churn out their software in a matter of days, and it's simple enough. The robot starts with a constructor in the class `Robot`:

```
public class Robot
{
   public Robot()
   {
   }
      .
      .
      .
}
```

And there are various actions that the robot can take, matched by methods of the same name in the `Robot` class — for example, to start the robot, you call the `start` method; to make the robot do its work by assembling a part (this robot is specialized to work on carburetors), call the `assemble` method; to test the installation of the part, call the `test` method, and so on.

```
public class Robot
{
   public Robot()
   {
   }

   public void start()
   {
      System.out.println("Starting....");
```

```
    }

    public void getParts()
    {
        System.out.println("Getting a carburetor....");
    }

    public void assemble()
    {
        System.out.println("Installing the carburetor....");
    }

    public void test()
    {
        System.out.println("Revving the engine....");
    }

    public void stop()
    {
        System.out.println("Stopping....");
    }
}
```

All that's needed is one method, called `go` here, which will make the robot do its work by calling the `start`, `getParts`, `assemble`, `test`, and `stop` methods:

```
public class Robot
{
    public Robot()
    {
    }

    public void go()
    {
        start();
        getParts();
        assemble();
        test();
        stop();
    }

    public void start()
    {
        System.out.println("Starting....");
    }

    public void getParts()
    {
```

```
      System.out.println("Getting a carburetor....");
   }

   public void assemble()
   {
     System.out.println("Installing the carburetor....");
   }

   public void test()
   {
     System.out.println("Revving the engine....");
   }

   public void stop()
   {
     System.out.println("Stopping....");
   }
}
```

You can quickly put together a test harness to check out the Robot class.
Just create a Robot object and call its go method to make the robot do its
work.

```
public class TestRobot
{
  public static void main(String args[])
  {
    Robot robot = new Robot();

    robot.go();
  }
}
```

And when you test the robot you get the following messages (much to the
CEO's delight):

```
Starting....
Getting a carburetor....
Installing the carburetor....
Revving the engine....
Stopping....
```

"Excellent!" cries the CEO. "Bonuses all around. I told you we didn't need any
of that darn design pattern stuff." The company programmers give you dirty
looks — and you happily collect your paycheck.

Creating Robots with the Template Method Pattern

"Good news!" cries the CEO of GigundoCorp, galloping into the break room the next day. "We landed that other contract!"

"What other contract?" everyone asks.

"The contract for a robot that bakes cookies," the CEO says. "Now get out there and create the software for it."

The company programmers look into their coffee cups. "We're going to have to rewrite all our software from scratch," they say.

The CEO glances at you from the corner of hooded eyes and asks, "Will it cost a lot?"

"Plenty," the company programmers say. And all this time you're resisting the temptation to say, "I told you so."

This is a good time to start talking about the Template Method design pattern. Here's the problem the GigundoCorp programmers face — they have an automotive robot class as shown in Figure 7-1:

Figure 7-1:
The
automotive
robot.

Automotive Robot

But now they need a cookie robot class as represented in Figure 7-2, and that class has to be written from scratch.

Figure 7-2:
The cookie
robot.

Cookie Robot

The cookie robot has a number of methods in common with the automotive robot, such as start and stop, but it needs to do different things as well — the assemble method should no longer display the message Getting a carburetor. . . ., for example; it should display a more appropriate message like Getting flour and sugar. . . .

That's where the Template Method pattern comes in. This pattern says you can write a method that defines a multi-step algorithm, just like the go method you've seen earlier in this chapter, which runs the multi-step algorithm corresponding to the robot's work.

```
public void go()
{
  start();
  getParts();
  assemble();
  test();
  stop();
}
```

Then you make this method into a template by allowing subclasses to redefine (in Java terms, *override*) various steps in this algorithm as needed. In this case, to build the cookie robot, for example, you'd override the getParts, assemble, and test methods.

According to the official Gang of Four (GoF) phrasing, the Template Method will "Define the skeleton of an algorithm in an operation, deferring some steps to subclasses. Template Method lets subclasses redefine certain steps of an algorithm without changing the algorithm's structure." (*Design Patterns: Elements of Reusable Object-Oriented Software,* 1995, Pearson Education, Inc. Publishing as Pearson Addison Wesley.)

So that means you should use the Template Method pattern when you have an algorithm that is made of up multiple steps, and you want to be able to customize some of those steps. Note that if you want to rewrite everything from scratch every time — if every step *has* to be customized by writing it from scratch — then you have no need of a template. Only if you have steps that are shared by various implementations of the algorithm do you need to work with a template.

Creating robots by template

If you had a template method to base robots on, you could make use of it in an inheriting class as illustrated in Figure 7-3:

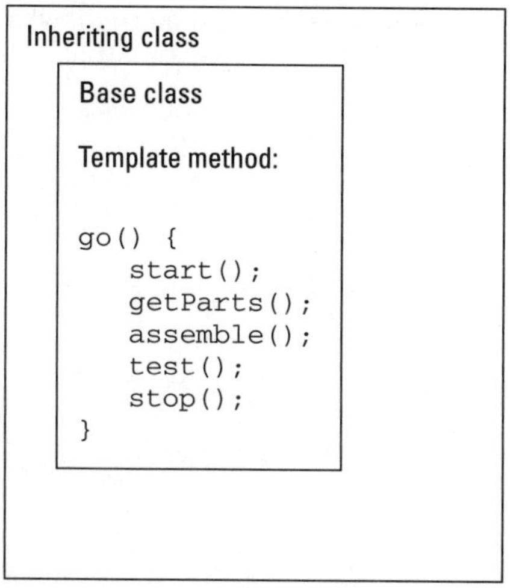

Figure 7-3:
Inheriting
from the
template
base class.

Inheriting class

Base class

Template method:

```
go() {
    start();
    getParts();
    assemble();
    test();
    stop();
}
```

By calling the go method, your multi-step algorithm is executed. To customize the inherited class, you only have to override the steps in the algorithm you want, like this in the cookie robot case (see Figure 7-4):

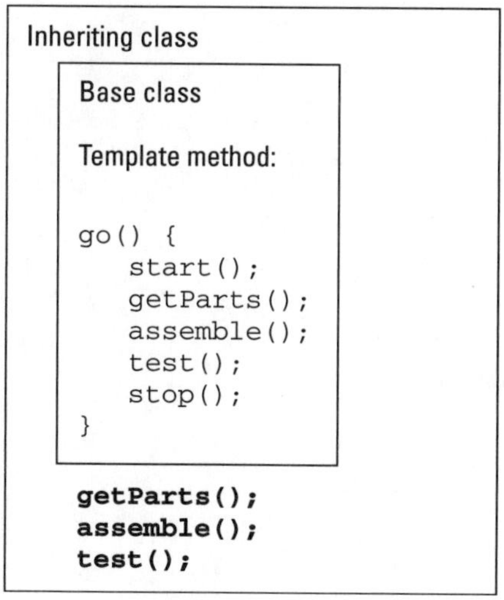

Figure 7-4:
Modifying
the inherited
methods.

Inheriting class

Base class

Template method:

```
go() {
    start();
    getParts();
    assemble();
    test();
    stop();
}
```

```
getParts();
assemble();
test();
```

That's the idea behind the Template Method design pattern — this method executes a multi-step algorithm that's customizable by subclasses. How's that going to look in the case of the two types of robots you need, automotive robots and cookie robots?

I start by putting the actual template method (the go method, which executes the work a robot has to do) in an abstract class (abstract so it has to be inherited), called RobotTemplate.

```
public abstract class RobotTemplate
{
  public final void go()
  {
    start();
    getParts();
    assemble();
    test();
    stop();
  }
  .
  .
  .
}
```

And this class will also have default implementations of each of the methods corresponding to the steps in the algorithm, start, getParts, assemble, test, and stop.

```
public abstract class RobotTemplate
{
  public final void go()
  {
    start();
    getParts();
    assemble();
    test();
    stop();
  }

  public void start()
  {
    System.out.println("Starting....");
  }

  public void getParts()
  {
    System.out.println("Getting parts....");
  }

  public void assemble()
  {
    System.out.println("Assembling....");
  }

  public void test()
```

```
  {
     System.out.println("Testing....");
  }

  public void stop()
  {
     System.out.println("Stopping....");
  }
}
```

If a robot is fine with any of these methods, such as the start and stop methods, it doesn't have to override them. Otherwise, you can customize what specific methods do in subclasses.

For example, say you want to use the RobotTemplate class to create an automotive robot. You'd start by extending the abstract RobotTemplate class in a new class, AutomotiveRobot.

```
public class AutomotiveRobot extends RobotTemplate
{
     .
     .
     .
}
```

The automotive robot should override a few of the RobotTemplate methods; for example, getParts should now display Getting a carburetor. . . ., assemble should now display Installing the carburetor. . . ., and test should display Revving the engine. . . ., so here's how you can customize the backbone multi-step algorithm provided by the template:

```
public class AutomotiveRobot extends RobotTemplate
{
  public void getParts()
  {
    System.out.println("Getting a carburetor....");
  }

  public void assemble()
  {
    System.out.println("Installing the carburetor....");
  }

  public void test()
  {
    System.out.println("Revving the engine....");
  }
}
```

You can also customize your template-based code by adding additional methods, such as a constructor that takes a name for the new robot and a `getName` method that returns that name.

```
public class AutomotiveRobot extends RobotTemplate
{
  private String name;

  public AutomotiveRobot(String n)
  {
    name = n;
  }

  public void getParts()
  {           .
    System.out.println("Getting a carburetor....");
  }

  public void assemble()
  {
    System.out.println("Installing the carburetor....");
  }

  public void test()
  {
    System.out.println("Revving the engine....");
  }

  public String getName()
  {
    return name;
  }
}
```

Excellent. You've used the inherited template `go` method and customized it for automotive robots.

You can also customize the inherited template method for cookie robots in a new class, `CookieRobot`, which also extends the `RobotTemplate` class. You can write the `CookieRobot` class by making the `getParts` method display `Getting flour and sugar. . . .`, the `assemble` method display `Baking a cookie. . . .`, and the `test` method display `Crunching a cookie. . . .`

```
public class CookieRobot extends RobotTemplate
{
  private String name;

  public CookieRobot(String n)
```

```
    {
        name = n;
    }

    public void getParts()
    {
        System.out.println("Getting flour and sugar....");
    }

    public void assemble()
    {
        System.out.println("Baking a cookie....");
    }

    public void test()
    {
        System.out.println("Crunching a cookie....");
    }

    public String getName()
    {
        return name;
    }
}
```

Now that you've used the go template method in two new classes, AutomotiveRobot and CookieRobot, and had to rewrite only those steps of the robot algorithm that differed between the two types of robots — you didn't have to rewrite these two classes from scratch.

Testing the creation of robots

Want to put this to the test? Run TestTemplate.java, which creates an object of the AutomotiveRobot and CookieRobot classes and calls the go method of each.

```
public class TestTemplate
{
    public static void main(String args[])
    {
        AutomotiveRobot automotiveRobot =
            new AutomotiveRobot("Automotive Robot");

        CookieRobot cookieRobot = new CookieRobot("Cookie Robot");

        System.out.println(automotiveRobot.getName() + ":");
        automotiveRobot.go();
```

```
    System.out.println();
    System.out.println(cookieRobot.getName() + ":");
    cookieRobot.go();
  }
}
```

When you run this test, you see that you have indeed been able to customize the multiple steps of the two types of robots' work algorithms.

```
Automotive Robot:
Starting....
Getting a carburetor....
Installing the carburetor....
Revving the engine....
Stopping....

Cookie Robot:
Starting....
Getting flour and sugar....
Baking a cookie....
Crunching a cookie....
Stopping....
```

Built-in Template Methods in Java

Any built-in uses of the Template Method design pattern come to mind in Java? Here's one — the update method built into Java to handle window refreshes. The update method is responsible for redrawing a window as needed, and it performs a well-defined sequence of steps. One of those steps, a call to the paint method, which is responsible for drawing the window's display, is available for overloading, and you've probably overloaded the paint method dozens of times. Bet you never thought you were using the Template Method design pattern.

There are many Java window classes that use the update method as a template method. For example, there's an update method in the JFrame class, and you can override the paint method called by update to do your own painting in a JFrame. Here's an example that displays a JFrame:

```java
import javax.swing.*;
import java.awt.*;
import java.awt.event.*;

public class Hello extends JFrame
{
    public Hello()
```

```
    {
        super("Hello Application");
    }

    public static void main(String args[])
    {
        final JFrame h = new Hello();

        h.setBounds(100, 100, 300, 300);
        h.setVisible(true);
        h.setDefaultCloseOperation(DISPOSE_ON_CLOSE);

        h.addWindowListener(new WindowAdapter() {
            public void windowClosing(WindowEvent e) {
                System.exit(0);
            }
        });
    }
}
```

All you're going to get here is an empty window, unless you do something more. And that's overriding the `paint` method this way, where I'm using the `Graphics` object passed to that method to write `No worries.` in the window.

```
import javax.swing.*;
import java.awt.*;
import java.awt.event.*;

public class Hello extends JFrame
{
    public Hello()
    {
        super("Hello Application");
    }

    public static void main(String args[])
    {
        final JFrame h = new Hello();

        h.setBounds(100, 100, 300, 300);
        h.setVisible(true);
        h.setDefaultCloseOperation(DISPOSE_ON_CLOSE);

        h.addWindowListener(new WindowAdapter() {
            public void windowClosing(WindowEvent e) {
                System.exit(0);
            }
        });
```

```
    }

    public void paint (Graphics g)
    {
        super.paint(g);
        g.drawString("No worries.", 60, 60);
    }
}
```

By overriding the paint method, you've changed one of the steps in the algorithm that displays your window.

Adding a hook

You can also provide *hooks* into your algorithm. A hook is a method that controls some aspect of that algorithm. For example, if you wanted to make the testing part of the Robot algorithm optional, you could surround that part with a conditional whose condition is set by a hook method named testOK.

```
public abstract class RobotHookTemplate
{
  public final void go()
  {
    start();
    getParts();
    assemble();
    if (testOK()){
      test();
    }
    stop();
  }

  public void start()
  {
    System.out.println("Starting....");
  }

  public void getParts()
  {
    System.out.println("Getting parts....");
  }

  public void assemble()
  {
    System.out.println("Assembling....");
  }

  public void test()
```

```
   {
      System.out.println("Testing....");
   }

   public void stop()
   {
      System.out.println("Stopping....");
   }

   public boolean testOK()
   {
      return true;
   }
}
```

By default, you can ignore the hook method `testOK` — if you do nothing with it, the Robot algorithm calls the full set of steps, including the `test` method. However, you can hook into the algorithm by overriding the `testOK` method in a subclass, like this in a new class, `CookieHookRobot`, where `testOK` returns `false`, not `true`.

```
public class CookieHookRobot extends RobotHookTemplate
{
   private String name;

   public CookieHookRobot(String n)
   {
      name = n;
   }

   public void getParts()
   {
      System.out.println("Getting flour and sugar....");
   }

   public void assemble()
   {
      System.out.println("Baking a cookie....");
   }

   public String getName()
   {
      return name;
   }

   public boolean testOK()
   {
      return false;
   }
}
```

Because the hook method `testOK` returns `false` now, the Robot algorithm will not call the `test` method, as you know from the `go` method.

```
public final void go()
{
  start();
  getParts();
  assemble();
  if (testOK()){
    test();
  }
  stop();
}
```

Testing the hook method

Now put this into a test harness, `TestHookTemplate.java`, and call the `cookieHookRobot.go` method.

```
public class TestHookTemplate
{
  public static void main(String args[])
  {
    CookieHookRobot cookieHookRobot =
      new CookieHookRobot("Cookie Robot");

    System.out.println(cookieHookRobot.getName() + ":");
    cookieHookRobot.go();
  }
}
```

You'll see the Robot algorithm at work — minus the test step:

```
Cookie Robot:
Starting....
Getting flour and sugar....
Baking a cookie....
Stopping....
```

There you have it — you didn't have to do anything with the hook, but if you did, you can affect the execution of the algorithm. If you build your algorithm using a succession of abstract methods, each of these methods has to be overridden in a subclass; hooks, on the other hand, don't have to be overridden at all, unless you want to change the default execution of the algorithm.

You use the Template Method design pattern when you've got an algorithm of several steps and you want to allow customization by subclasses. It's that easy. Implement the steps in that algorithm as an overridable method calls in an abstract class, and let the subclasses override those steps as required.

The Template Method pattern is great when you have a multi-step algorithm to implement that you also want to customize. There's an allied pattern that does much the same thing that I take a look at in the next section, called the Builder pattern.

Building Robots with the Builder Pattern

"Good news!" cries the CEO of GigundoCorp, trotting into the break room. "Our customers have told us that they want more control over what actions a robot will perform, so we can't use a pre-written template method anymore. Now they want to be able to pick and choose each action the robot will perform."

"Let me get this straight," you say. "The way we've set things up, robots start, get parts, assemble, test, and then stop. But now customers want to control the order and number of those commands? So a robot might start, then test, then assemble, then stop?"

"Right," says the CEO.

"Time for a new design pattern," you say.

"I was afraid of that," says the CEO.

The client rules

In the Template Method design pattern, the multi-step algorithm is king — you set it up the way you want it, and all the subclasses have to follow your lead. But now the situation is different — the client wants to set the order and number of steps in the algorithm. So the code you develop will no longer be central, as it was, and will have to be encapsulated in a new class — a builder class.

The Template Method pattern you saw earlier in this chapter lets you customize the steps of a multi-step algorithm by overriding the steps in that algorithm as you can see in Figure 7-5.

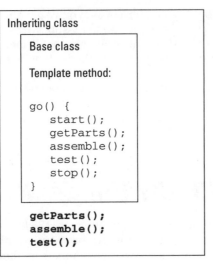

Figure 7-5:
The
Template
Method
pattern
allows you
to customize
the multi-
step
algorithm.

Everything is based on the template method in this design pattern, and you can customize that template as needed. But now you no longer have control over the algorithm — the client does, and it constructs a robot by specifying which actions, and in which order, the robot should execute. For example, to add a start action, the client code might call an addStart method. To add a test action, it might call an addTest method, and so on as shown in Figure 7-6.

Figure 7-6:
Customizing
client code
with an
addStart
method.

```
Client code

addStart
addTest
addAssemble
addStop
```

Being able to specify the actions the robot under construction should exe-cute, and in what order, is now under the control of the GigundoCorp cus-tomer. So your code now moves to a new class, the CookieRobotBuilder class, which is the class that supports the addStart, addTest, addAssemble, and addStop methods as shown in Figure 7-7.

Figure 7-7:
Separating
out the
construction
code into
the Cookie
Robot
Builder
class.

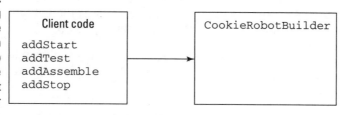

So the client code uses the `CookieRobotBuilder` to build a cookie robot. When the client code is done building the robot, it calls the `CookieRobot Builder getRobot` method to get the newly built robot, as illustrated in Figure 7-8.

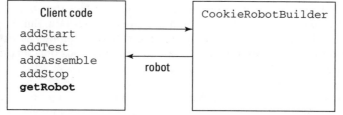

Figure 7-8:
Sending the
robot to the
client code.

What if the client code wanted to build an automotive robot instead, giving that robot the same sequence of actions? In that case, all it would have to do is to use an `AutomotiveRobotBuilder` object instead, as shown in Figure 7-9.

Figure 7-9:
Using the
Automotive
Robot
Builder
class for
construction
instead of
the Cookie
Robot
Builder
class.

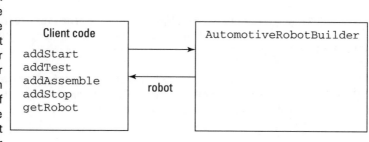

So now that the client code has taken over the specification of the algorithm, you don't inherit a template method anymore and then customize that method to create your own robots. Instead, to create different types of robots, you allow client code to use different builder objects.

That's the idea: the client code now sets the sequence and number of the steps in the algorithm, and selects which builders to use to create the robot it wants.

After the sequence and number of steps have been set up in the client code, that code can use them over and over, creating all kinds of different robots — all it has to do is to switch between various builders. And that's what the Builder design pattern is all about.

The GoF says that the Builder design patterns let you "Separate the construction of a complex object from its representation so that the same construction processes can create different representations."

The main difference between the Template Method and the Builder design patterns is in who creates the sequence of steps in the algorithm. In the Template Method, you do, and subclasses can make alterations. In the Builder pattern, the client code sets the sequence and number of steps in the algorithm and swaps between the builders you provide to create various objects that embody that algorithm.

Use the Builder design pattern when you want client code to have control over the construction process but want to be able to end up with different kinds of objects (each of which is built by a different type of builder). For example, this is the pattern you want when you're building robots using the same construction process but want to be able to end up with different kinds of robots — all the client code has to do is to load different builders; the construction process stays the same. Here's another example — you might want to take a text stream and build a document from it but be able to create documents in various formats, such as RTF, Microsoft Word, plain text, and so on. Although the construction process is the same for each document, you use a different builder for each *type* of document.

In other words, when the client code has control over the construction process but you still want to be able to construct different kinds of objects, the Builder design pattern should spring to mind.

This pattern is similar to the Factory pattern, also one of the GoF patterns, but the Factory pattern can be more involved, and it centers on a single-step creation process, not a configurable sequence of steps, as here.

Letting clients build robots

When you use the Builder pattern, the client code is in charge of the construction process, and it's up to your builders to do what the client code wants. To let the client build robots to perform various sequences of actions — starting, assembling, stopping, and so on — I make the RobotBuilder interface support these methods: addStart, addGetParts, addAssemble, addTest, and addStop.

For example, to make the robot under construction start, test, assemble, and then stop, the client code only needs to call the builder's addStart, addTest, addAssemble, and addStop methods, in that order. When the robot has been constructed, the client code only needs to call the builder's getRobot method to get the new robot. And the new robot object will support a go method that, when called, executes the sequence of actions it's been constructed to run.

Because you can have multiple types of robot builders — those that build cookie robots or automotive robots, for example — I start by creating a RobotBuilder interface that all robot builders have to implement. This interface lists the methods that all robot builders must implement, from addStart to addStop, as well as the getRobot method:

```
public interface RobotBuilder
{
  public void addStart();
  public void addGetParts();
  public void addAssemble();
  public void addTest();
  public void addStop();
  public RobotBuildable getRobot();
}
```

I start by creating the cookie robot builder, CookieRobotBuilder, which, as all robot builders must, implements the RobotBuilder interface.

```
public class CookieRobotBuilder implements RobotBuilder
{
    .
    .
    .
}
```

The robot that the code will build is based on the CookieRobotBuildable class, coming up in the "Creating some buildable robots" section. The constructed robot is going to be a CookieRobotBuildable object, so we'll need an object of that class in the builder (this is the object the builder will return as the fully constructed robot):

```
public class CookieRobotBuilder implements RobotBuilder
{
  CookieRobotBuildable robot;

  public CookieRobotBuilder()
  {
    robot = new CookieRobotBuildable();
  }
      .
      .
      .
}
```

The client code can add robot actions like start, stop, test, assemble, getParts, and so on in any order, and each action can be added any number of times. To keep track of the sequence of actions the client code wants to build into the current robot, I use an `ArrayList` object named `actions` in the builder.

```
import java.util.*;

public class CookieRobotBuilder implements RobotBuilder
{
  CookieRobotBuildable robot;
  ArrayList<Integer> actions;

  public CookieRobotBuilder()
  {
    robot = new CookieRobotBuildable();
    actions = new ArrayList<Integer>();
  }
      .
      .
      .
}
```

An easy way of storing the action sequence in the `actions` `ArrayList` as it's built by the client code is to assign an integer for each action, as shown in the following:

- ✔ start = 1
- ✔ getParts = 2
- ✔ assemble = 3, and so on

I store `Integer` objects in the `ArrayList`. For example, when the client code wants to add a start action, it calls `addStart`, making the robot builder add an `Integer` object containing 1 to the `actions` `ArrayList`, and so on. Here are all the methods that add actions to the robot in the builder:

```java
import java.util.*;

public class CookieRobotBuilder implements RobotBuilder
{
  CookieRobotBuildable robot;
  ArrayList<Integer> actions;

  public CookieRobotBuilder()
  {
    robot = new CookieRobotBuildable();
    actions = new ArrayList<Integer>();
  }

  public void addStart()
  {
    actions.add(new Integer(1));
  }

  public void addGetParts()
  {
    actions.add(new Integer(2));
  }

  public void addAssemble()
  {
    actions.add(new Integer(3));
  }

  public void addTest()
  {
    actions.add(new Integer(4));
  }

  public void addStop()
  {
    actions.add(new Integer(5));
  }

    .
    .
    .
}
```

When the client code wants to get the robot object it has configured from the builder, it calls the builder's getRobot method. When that method is called, you know the construction process is complete, so you can configure the robot by passing it the ArrayList of actions it should execute. In this example, each robot can be configured by passing the ArrayList to the robot's loadActions method; after the robot is configured, it's returned by the getRobot method in the builder.

```
import java.util.*;

public class CookieRobotBuilder implements RobotBuilder
{
  CookieRobotBuildable robot;
  ArrayList<Integer> actions;

  public CookieRobotBuilder()
  {
    robot = new CookieRobotBuildable();
    actions = new ArrayList<Integer>();
  }

  public void addStart()
  {
    actions.add(new Integer(1));
  }
        .
        .
        .
  public void addStop()
  {
    actions.add(new Integer(5));
  }

  public RobotBuildable getRobot()
  {
    robot.loadActions(actions);
    return robot;
  }
}
```

That completes the builder, which lets the client code configure the robot by
adding various actions — as many, and in whatever order, as required. So
how about creating the Robot class that the robots will be based on?

Creating some buildable robots

Each type of builder builds a different type of robot, and each robot is based
on its own class, such as the CookieRobotBuildable or Automotive
RobotBuildable class. All robots have to have a go method to make them
execute their actions, so you might start with an interface, RobotBuildable,
that makes sure that the go method is implemented in all robots.

```
public interface RobotBuildable
{
  public void go();
}
```

Now all `Robot` classes will implement this interface. Here's how the `Cookie RobotBuildable` class, which you make cookie robot objects out of, works. You can load the robot with the `ArrayList` of actions that it's supposed to execute into an `ArrayList` named `actions` in the `loadActions` method, which is called by the robot builder to configure this robot.

```java
import java.util.*;

public class CookieRobotBuildable implements RobotBuildable
{
  ArrayList<Integer> actions;

  public CookieRobotBuildable()
  {
  }

  public void loadActions(ArrayList a)
  {
    actions = a;
  }
      .
      .
      .
}
```

When the client code wants the robot to perform the actions it's been built to perform, that code calls the robot's `go` method. In the `go` method, you can iterate over the `actions` `ArrayList` and call the methods corresponding to the actions that have been built into the robot. For example, unpacking a 1 from the `ArrayList` means you should call the `start` method, unpacking a 2 means you should call the `getParts` method, and so on. You can handle this with an `Iterator` object and a `switch` statement in the robot's `go` method, as shown in the following code:

```java
import java.util.*;

public class CookieRobotBuildable implements RobotBuildable
{
  ArrayList<Integer> actions;

  public CookieRobotBuildable()
  {
  }

  public final void go()
  {
    Iterator itr = actions.iterator();
```

```
      while(itr.hasNext()) {
        switch ((Integer)itr.next()){
          case 1:
            start();
            break;
          case 2:
            getParts();
            break;
          case 3:
            assemble();
            break;
          case 4:
            test();
            break;
          case 5:
            stop();
            break;
        }
      }
    }
      .
      .
      .

    public void loadActions(ArrayList a)
    {
      actions = a;
    }
}
```

You have to add the methods for each action as well: The start method
(displays Starting. . . .), the getParts method (displays Getting
flour and sugar. . . ., for a cookie robot), and so on.

```
import java.util.*;

public class CookieRobotBuildable implements RobotBuildable
{
  ArrayList<Integer> actions;

  public CookieRobotBuildable()
  {
  }

  public final void go()
  {
    Iterator itr = actions.iterator();

    while(itr.hasNext()) {
      switch ((Integer)itr.next()){
```

```java
        case 1:
          start();
          break;
        case 2:
          getParts();
          break;
        case 3:
          assemble();
          break;
        case 4:
          test();
          break;
        case 5:
          stop();
          break;
      }
    }
  }

public void start()
{
  System.out.println("Starting....");
}

public void getParts()
{
  System.out.println("Getting flour and sugar....");
}

public void assemble()
{
  System.out.println("Baking a cookie....");
}

public void test()
{
  System.out.println("Crunching a cookie....");
}

public void stop()
{
  System.out.println("Stopping....");
}

public void loadActions(ArrayList a)
{
  actions = a;
}
}
```

That completes the `CookieRobotBuildable` class. Now you've got the robot builder and the robot; all you need is the client code that will actually configure the robot as it wants.

Because the builder and the robot are both based on interfaces, the client code can be independent of the type of builder or robot it wants. The construction code can stay the same no matter what builder and what robot are required. The only place where it matters which builder you want to use is where you actually load that builder.

Testing the robot builder

The test harness, `TestRobotBuilder.java`, acts as the client code. That code lets the user decide what type of robot to build with the following prompt: `Do you want a cookie robot [c] or an automotive one [a]?`

```
import java.io.*;

public class TestRobotBuilder
{
  public static void main(String args[])
  {
    String response = "a";

    System.out.print(
      "Do you want a cookie robot [c] or an automotive one [a]? ");
    BufferedReader reader = new
      BufferedReader(new InputStreamReader(System.in));

    try{
      response = reader.readLine();
    } catch (IOException e){
      System.err.println("Error");
    }
      .
      .
      .
  }
```

Depending on which type of robot the user selects, a cookie robot builder or an automotive robot builder is created and stored in the `RobotBuilder` variable builder. (Note that the rest of the code is independent of the type of builder and robot you're using.)

```
import java.io.*;

public class TestRobotBuilder
{
  public static void main(String args[])
  {
    RobotBuilder builder;
    String response = "a";

    System.out.print(
      "Do you want a cookie robot [c] or an automotive one [a]? ");
    BufferedReader reader = new
      BufferedReader(new InputStreamReader(System.in));

    try{
      response = reader.readLine();
    } catch (IOException e){
      System.err.println("Error");
    }

    if (response.equals("c")){
      builder = new CookieRobotBuilder();
    } else {
      builder = new AutomotiveRobotBuilder();
    }
      .
      .
      .
  }
}
```

Then this client code can construct the robot as it wants, using the builder's addStart, addGetParts, addAssemble, addTest, and addStop methods, which it can use in any order.

```
import java.io.*;

public class TestRobotBuilder
{
  public static void main(String args[])
  {
    RobotBuilder builder;
    String response = "a";

    System.out.print(
      "Do you want a cookie robot [c] or an automotive one [a]? ");
    BufferedReader reader = new
      BufferedReader(new InputStreamReader(System.in));
```

```
    try{
      response = reader.readLine();
    } catch (IOException e){
      System.err.println("Error");
    }

    if (response.equals("c")){
      builder = new CookieRobotBuilder();
    } else {
      builder = new AutomotiveRobotBuilder();
    }

    //Start the construction process.

    builder.addStart();
    builder.addTest();
    builder.addAssemble();
    builder.addStop();
        .
        .
        .
  }
}
```

After the robot has been built, the client code calls the builder's getRobot method, which returns a robot stored in a RobotBuildable variable. And you can call the robot's go method to make sure it does what it's supposed to.

```
import java.io.*;

public class TestRobotBuilder
{
  public static void main(String args[])
  {
    RobotBuilder builder;
    RobotBuildable robot;
    String response = "a";

    System.out.print(
      "Do you want a cookie robot [c] or an automotive one [a]? ");
    BufferedReader reader = new
      BufferedReader(new InputStreamReader(System.in));

    try{
      response = reader.readLine();
    } catch (IOException e){
      System.err.println("Error");
    }
```

```
  if (response.equals("c")){
    builder = new CookieRobotBuilder();
  } else {
    builder = new AutomotiveRobotBuilder();
  }

  //Start the construction process.

  builder.addStart();
  builder.addTest();
  builder.addAssemble();
  builder.addStop();

  robot = builder.getRobot();

  robot.go();
 }
}
```

This client code can produce cookie robots or automotive robots simply by selecting the right builder. Here, it is creating a cookie robot:

```
Do you want a cookie robot [c] or an automotive one [a]? c
Starting....
Crunching a cookie....
Baking a cookie....
Stopping....
```

And here it is creating an automotive robot, using the same construction sequence:

```
Do you want a cookie robot [c] or an automotive one [a]? a
Starting....
Revving the engine....
Installing the carburetor....
Stopping....
```

Not bad. You've put builders to work to let client code take control over the construction process.

Chapter 8

Handling Collections with the Iterator and Composite Patterns

● ●

In This Chapter

▶ Using the Iterator pattern

▶ Creating iterators

▶ Iterating over vice presidents using a home-grown iterator

▶ Understanding the Composite pattern

▶ Using iterators inside composites

▶ Parsing XML documents using the Composite pattern

● ●

*T*he CEO of GiantDataPool Inc., the new corporation you're consulting for, sidles into your cubicle and says something inaudible.

"What?" you ask.

The CEO looks around with a haunted expression and says, "I have a top-secret project for you."

"Top secret?" you ask. "What's it about?"

"Not so loud!" whispers the CEO. "We need an outsider for this project, so I'm coming to you. It seems that we've got some administrative bloat going on, and we need to track our vice presidents — no one knows how many there are now. There seems, um, to be about twice as many vice presidents as programmers now."

"Too much management, not enough programmers," you sigh. "The typical corporate story."

"We want to start with the Sales division," the CEO whispers. "Can you write a program that loops over all the VPs and prints them all out?"

"Better than that," you say. "I'll use the Iterator pattern."

This chapter is about two allied design patterns: the Iterator pattern and the Composite pattern. The Iterator pattern gives you a way of accessing the elements inside an object without having to know the internal details of that object. For example, Sun has introduced all kinds of collections in Java relatively recently, and these collections allow you to create *iterators* — special objects designed to give you access to the members of a collection — for easy access.

The Composite design pattern is also about collections. With the Composite pattern, the idea is that you can create tree-like structures where each item in the tree — a single leaf with no children, or an entire branch with many children — can be handled in the same way. The Composite pattern is designed to let you handle different types of objects in the same collection in the same way, and iterators fit in naturally here — to handle the elements of a tree branch, for example, you can iterate over them. You learn how to make the most of both these patterns in this chapter.

Accessing Objects with the Iterator Pattern

When you're dealing with a collection of objects, the Iterator pattern is the ideal solution. These days, you have all kinds of collections to work with — trees, binary trees, arrays, ring buffers, hashes, hash maps, array lists, and many more. The ways these collections store their data internally vary a great deal, and if you want to access that data in the same way as these collections do internally, you have to learn a different technique for every collection type.

That's where the Interator pattern comes in. You can use a well-defined interface of methods to access the elements of a collection. Over the years, those standard methods have become widely adopted, and they appear throughout this chapter. Using those methods, you can access the elements in collections in a standard way.

According to the Gang of Four (GoF), you can use the Iterator design pattern to "Provide a way to access the elements of an aggregate object sequentially without exposing its underlying representation." (*Design Patterns: Elements of Reusable Object-Oriented Software,* 1995, Pearson Education, Inc. Publishing as Pearson Addison Wesley).

In other words, iterators are designed to let you handle many different kinds of collections by accessing their members in a standard, accepted way, without having to know the internal details of those collections.

The Iterator design pattern is especially important when the collection you're creating is made up internally of separate subcollections, as when you've mixed hashes with array lists, for example.

Iterators are usually written in Java as standalone classes. Why aren't iterators built into the collections they work with? They could be, but in Java and other languages, they're not. The design insight here is one of what's called *single responsibility* — a class should have only one thing to do. The thinking is that the collection maintains the collection; the iterator provides access to the elements of the collection. Separating responsibilities between classes is useful when a class has to change — if there's too much going on in a single class, it's going to be too hard to rewrite. When change has to happen, a single class should have only one reason to change.

Accessing your objects with an iterator

You start to work on the CEO's problem of tracking vice presidents. In this case, you decide to store the vice presidents in a collection, with a set of methods that provide access to the VPs. In the early days of iterators, the classic methods that iterators were supposed to implement were the following:

- ✔ was
- ✔ first
- ✔ next
- ✔ isDone
- ✔ currentItem

In Java today, however, iterators follow the lead of the `java.util.Iterator` interface, which defines these three methods:

- ✔ next
- ✔ hasNext
- ✔ remove

The `next` method returns the `next` element in the collection, `hasNext` returns `true` if there are additional elements in the collection and `false` otherwise, and `remove` allows you to remove an element from the collection.

That's how iterators work — they provide a simple, consistent interface for working with various collections. Suppose that client code is faced with a complex, terrifying collection (as represented in Figure 8-1) and doesn't know how to work with it.

Figure 8-1:
Client code facing a complex and terrifying collection.

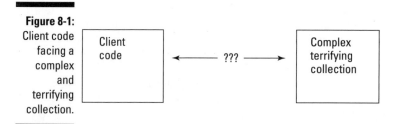

The client code can get an iterator to smooth out the interface with the collection, and the client code can use the iterator's standard methods to interact with the collection, as shown in Figure 8-2:

Figure 8-2:
Using an iterator to handle a collection.

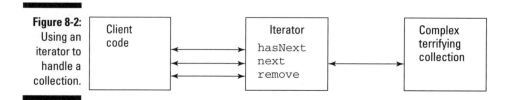

The first order of business to deal with the vice president problem is to store the vice presidents in some way. You decide to start by creating a class that stores each VP's information in a class named VP.

You must create the following four important components for this class:

- ✔ The constructor to which you pass the name of the VP.
- ✔ The name of the division in which the VP works.
- ✔ A `getName` method to return the name of the VP.
- ✔ A `print` method that prints the VP's info, including both the VP's name and division.

```
public class VP
{
  private String name;
  private String division;

  public VP(String n, String d)
  {
    name = n;
    division = d;
  }

  public String getName()
  {
    return name;
  }

  public void print()
  {
    System.out.println("Name: " + name + " Division: " + division);
  }

}
```

That encapsulates individual vice presidents. Now you've got to store all the vice presidents in a collection.

Gathering the vice presidents into a collection

In this example, I base the collection of vice presidents on a simple Java array. The reason for that is that any more substantial Java collection, such as a vector, array list, hash map, or so on, already has an `iterator` method built in that returns you a handy iterator, so creating an iterator from scratch to work with the collection seems a little silly.

You decide to store the vice presidents in a division, such as `Sales`, in a class named `Division`.

```
public class Division
{
    .
    .
    .
}
```

The `Division` constructor stores the name of the division, such as `Sales`, and the `getNames` method returns that name.

```
public class Division
{
  private String name;

  public Division(String n)
  {
    name = n;
  }

  public String getName()
  {
    return name;
  }
    .
    .
    .
}
```

The vice presidents are stored in an array of `vP` objects named `vPs`, and you can add a new vice president to that array with the `add` method, as shown in the following code:

```
public class Division
{
  private VP[] VPs = new VP[100];
  private int number = 0;
  private String name;

  public Division(String n)
  {
    name = n;
  }

  public String getName()
  {
    return name;
  }

  public void add(String n)
  {
    VP vp = new VP(n, name);
    VPs[number++] = vp;
  }
    .
    .
    .
}
```

In other words, the `Division` object is the collection, and the `VP` objects are the elements in the collection. To add an iterator, the collection should have a method — the name is up to you, perhaps something like `iterator` (possible names include `createIterator` and `getIterator`). This method passes the array of vice presidents to the constructor of the `iterator` class, `DivisionIterator`, and returns a newly-created `DivisionIterator` object.

```java
public class Division
{
  private VP[] VPs = new VP[100];
  private int number = 0;
  private String name;

  public Division(String n)
  {
    name = n;
  }

  public String getName()
  {
    return name;
  }

  public void add(String n)
  {
    VP vp = new VP(n, name);
    VPs[number++] = vp;
  }

  public DivisionIterator iterator()
  {
    return new DivisionIterator(VPs);
  }

}
```

The next step is to create the iterator itself, the `DivisionIterator` class, that lets you iterate over the vice presidents stored in the collection.

Creating the iterator

The iterator class, `DivisionIterator`, implements the three `java.util.Iterator` methods: `next`, `hasNext`, and `remove`. You start this way by implementing the `Iterator` interface:

```java
import java.util.Iterator;

public class DivisionIterator implements Iterator
{
```

```
      .
      .
      .
}
```

The constructor accepts the array of VP objects and stores it:

```
import java.util.Iterator;

public class DivisionIterator implements Iterator
{
  private VP[] VPs;

  public DivisionIterator(VP[] v)
  {
    VPs = v;
  }
      .
      .
      .
}
```

Now you've got to implement the Iterator interface methods to make this class into an iterator. The next method returns the next element in the array, and that's easy enough to do if you keep track of your present location in the array.

```
import java.util.Iterator;

public class DivisionIterator implements Iterator
{
  private VP[] VPs;
  private int location = 0;

  public DivisionIterator(VP[] v)
  {
    VPs = v;
  }

  public VP next()
  {
    return VPs[location++];
  }
      .
      .
      .
}
```

The hasNext method should return true if there is a next element in the array that hasn't been read so far, and false otherwise. In this case, you have to check not only if you're at the end of the array, but also because you're dealing with a fixed-length array, you have to check if the next element is null — if it is, that array element is empty. Here's what the hasNext method looks like:

```java
import java.util.Iterator;

public class DivisionIterator implements Iterator
{
  private VP[] VPs;
  private int location = 0;

  public DivisionIterator(VP[] v)
  {
    VPs = v;
  }

  public VP next()
  {
    return VPs[location++];
  }

  public boolean hasNext()
  {
    if(location < VPs.length && VPs[location] != null){
      return true;
    } else {
      return false;
    }
  }
      .
      .
      .
}
```

In this case, you're interested in treating the vice presidents array as read-only, so you might add an empty implementation for the remove method.

```java
import java.util.Iterator;

public class DivisionIterator implements Iterator
{
  private VP[] VPs;
  private int location = 0;

  public DivisionIterator(VP[] v)
  {
```

```
    VPs = v;
  }

  public VP next()
  {
    return VPs[location++];
  }

  public boolean hasNext()
  {
    if(location < VPs.length && VPs[location] != null){
      return true;
    } else {
      return false;
    }
  }

  public void remove()
  {
  }
}
```

Excellent. You've got vice president objects, a division that represents a collection of vice presidents, and an iterator. All that's left is to put this all to work and start iterating over vice presidents.

Iterating over vice presidents

To test this out, all you've got to do is to create a division, stock it with some vice presidents, and then iterate over those vice presidents. That all happens in the test harness, TestDivision.java.

```
public class TestDivision
{
  public static void main(String args[])
  {
    TestDivision d = new TestDivision();
  }

  public TestDivision()
  {
    .
    .
    .
}
```

The code starts by creating the corporate Sales division and adding some vice presidents:

```
public class TestDivision
{
  Division division;

  public static void main(String args[])
  {
    TestDivision d = new TestDivision();
  }

  public TestDivision()
  {
    division = new Division("Sales");

    division.add("Ted");
    division.add("Bob");
    division.add("Carol");
    division.add("Alice");
        .
        .
        .

  }
}
```

Then it creates a `Division` class iterator by calling the `iterator` method and uses the `hasNext` and `next` methods to loop over the collection of vice presidents, displaying each one.

```
public class TestDivision
{
  Division division;
  DivisionIterator iterator;

  public static void main(String args[])
  {
    TestDivision d = new TestDivision();
  }

  public TestDivision()
  {
    division = new Division("Sales");

    division.add("Ted");
    division.add("Bob");
    division.add("Carol");
    division.add("Alice");
```

```
    iterator = division.iterator();

    while (iterator.hasNext()){
      VP vp = iterator.next();
      vp.print();
    }
  }
}
```

And sure enough, it prints out the full list of vice presidents.

```
Name: Ted Division: Sales
Name: Bob Division: Sales
Name: Carol Division: Sales
Name: Alice Division: Sales
```

Java itself, of course, comes stocked with plenty of iterators, especially in its new collection classes. You can see an example using one of the built-in iterators in Java in Chapter 7, where you iterate over an ArrayList when constructing a robot whose actions can be configured and stored at runtime. The code looks like this:

```
import java.util.*;

public class CookieRobotBuildable implements RobotBuildable
{
  ArrayList<Integer> actions;

  public CookieRobotBuildable()
  {
  }

  public final void go()
  {
    Iterator itr = actions.iterator();

    while(itr.hasNext()) {
      switch ((Integer)itr.next()){
        case 1:
          start();
          break;
        case 2:
          getParts();
          break;
        case 3:
          assemble();
          break;
        case 4:
          test();
```

```
            break;
        case 5:
            stop();
            break;
        }
    }
}

public void start()
{
    System.out.println("Starting....");
}

public void getParts()
{
    System.out.println("Getting flour and sugar....");
}

public void assemble()
{
    System.out.println("Baking a cookie....");
}

public void test()
{
    System.out.println("Crunching a cookie....");
}

public void stop()
{
    System.out.println("Stopping....");
}

public void loadActions(ArrayList a)
{
    actions = a;
}
}
```

In Java, iterators are everywhere. The `Iterator` interface is the basis of the `Collection`, `ListIterator`, and `Enumeration` interfaces, and they're implemented all over the place. Here's a partial list of classes that implement the `Collection` interface. (Take a deep breath before reading this aloud.)

- ✔ AbstractCollection
- ✔ AbstractList
- ✔ AbstractQueue
- ✔ AbstractSequentialList
- ✔ AbstractSet
- ✔ ArrayBlockingQueue
- ✔ ArrayList
- ✔ AttributeList

- ✔ BeanContextServices Support
- ✔ BeanContextSupport
- ✔ ConcurrentLinkedQueue
- ✔ CopyOnWriteArrayList
- ✔ CopyOnWriteArraySet
- ✔ DelayQueue
- ✔ EnumSet
- ✔ HashSet
- ✔ JobStateReasons
- ✔ LinkedBlockingQueue
- ✔ LinkedHashSet
- ✔ LinkedList
- ✔ PriorityBlockingQueue
- ✔ PriorityQueue
- ✔ RoleList
- ✔ RoleUnresolvedList
- ✔ Stack
- ✔ SynchronousQueue
- ✔ TreeSet
- ✔ Vector

More fun with for/in

Java 5 makes working with iterators all the more easy by making them disappear entirely. You can do that with the for/in statement. For example, say you have an ArrayList named VPs that stores vice president names as strings. You could use this code to print out each one:

```
for (String vp: VPs){
    System.out.println(vp);
}
```

For each iteration of the loop over the VPs collection, the String variable vp holds the current vice president's name, and you can print it out as shown. Here's how to use this loop in context in an example application, TestForIn.java, which creates an ArrayList of strings to store the names of the VPs and then loops over that ArrayList:

```
import java.util.*;

public class TestForIn
{
    ArrayList<String> VPs;

    public static void main(String args[])
    {
        TestForIn t = new TestForIn();
```

```
    }

    public TestForIn()
    {
      VPs = new ArrayList<String>();

      VPs.add("Ted");
      VPs.add("Bob");
      VPs.add("Carol");
      VPs.add("Alice");

      for (String vp: VPs){
        System.out.println(vp);
      }
    }
  }
```

Putting Together Composites

The CEO of GiantDataPool Inc. hurtles into your cubicle jubilantly and cries, "I like firing vice presidents!"

"Good," you say.

"I want to do more. Now I need a printout of all the vice presidents in the company — not just the Sales division, but all divisions."

"All divisions?" you ask.

"Yep. And there are some vice presidents just floating around independently, not even connected to a division."

"Hmm," you say, "this is going to take a new design pattern."

"Hey wait," says the CEO. "Remember that this is supposed to be a cost-cutting measure."

"I'll use the Composite pattern," you say.

"Is it expensive?"

"No," you say, "but I am."

You understand the problem — now you have to handle the whole corporation, not just a single division. The corporation has divisions with VPs — and divisions can contain other divisions — as well as free-floating VPs. Yipes. Figure 8-3 shows what the corporation looks like:

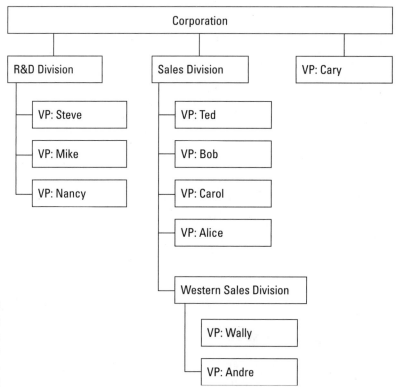

Figure 8-3:
All the parts
of the
corporation.

So now you've got a complex organization to work with, not just the simple Sales division. And the CEO wants to be able to print out the whole structure, so not only should each VP object have a `print` method, but each division should have a `print` method too. Okay, it's time for the Composite pattern.

You want to have a `print` method that can be called to print out a vice president, a division, or the whole corporation. The Composite pattern is all about creating tree-like structures where the leaves in a structure can be treated in the same way as the branches (which are substructures that can contain multiple leaves, as well as other branches). The idea here is that, to make life easier, you should be able to treat the leaves and compositions of leaves in a tree structure the same.

The GoF says you use the Composite design pattern to "Compose objects into tree structures to represent part-whole hierarchies. Composite lets clients treat individual objects and compositions of objects uniformly."

That's what you need here — a design pattern that lets you treat the leaves and branches of a tree structure equally because you want to be able to print out all the vice presidents individually, in a division, or in the whole corporation, just by calling the print method.

The Composite design pattern fits in with the Iterator pattern because when you ask each division to print itself, it can simply iterate over each vice president. That's typical of the Composite pattern — when you ask a branch to perform some action, it iterates over all its contained leaves and branches.

The insight behind the Composite pattern is really about treating the leaves and branches in a tree-like structure the same way, not about tree structures per se. That makes it a heck of a lot easier to work with complex structures like trees because you don't have to use a different set of methods with a part of the structure compared to the whole.

To implement the Composite pattern, the GoF suggests that you use an abstract class as the basis for both the leaves and branches in the tree. Doing so gives the leaves and branches a common set of methods, which is what the Composite pattern is all about. The GoF suggests an abstract class, but you can also use an interface for this job in Java.

It all starts with an abstract class

I'll stick with the GoF suggestion and create an abstract class that both vice presidents and divisions will implement, the Corporate class. Here's what it looks like — note that it has an add method, an iterator method to return an iterator over any contained vice presidents, and a print method:

```
import java.util.*;

public abstract class Corporate
{
  public String getName()
  {
    return "";
  }

  public void add(Corporate c)
  {
  }
}
```

```
    public Iterator iterator()
    {
      return null;
    }

    public void print()
    {
    }
}
```

This is the class that both the vice president leaves and the division branches in the corporation will extend.

Creating the vice president leaves

The VP class you created earlier in this chapter has to be modified a little so that you can unify the way you deal with both vice presidents and divisions in the corporate tree, as the Composite pattern says you should. In particular, you have to base the VP class on the common Corporate abstract class you created in the previous section.

```
import java.util.*;

public class VP extends Corporate
{
      .
      .
      .
}
```

The actual guts of the VP class are much as before — you just store the VP's name and division, and the print method prints out that information. But to let client code treat VPs the same way as it treats divisions, you can add a new iterator method to return an iterator. Because VPs don't contain other VPs, the returned iterator returns the current VP object only when you call the next method, and the hasNext method always returns false. Here's how you add the iterator method to the VP class, which returns a new iterator of the VPIterator class:

```
import java.util.*;

public class VP extends Corporate
{
  private String name;
  private String division;

  public VP(String n, String d)
  {
```

```
    name = n;
    division = d;
  }

  public String getName()
  {
    return name;
  }

  public void print()
  {
    System.out.println("Name: " + name + " Division: " + division);
  }

  public Iterator iterator()
  {
    return new VPIterator(this);
  }

}
```

What's the VPIterator class look like? That's easy enough — in this class, you just implement the Java Iterator interface, pass the VP object the iterator it should work with to its constructor, have the next method return that object, and the hasNext method return false, as shown in the following code:

```
import java.util.Iterator;

public class VPIterator implements Iterator
{
  private VP vp;

  public VPIterator(VP v)
  {
    vp = v;
  }

  public VP next()
  {
    return vp;
  }

  public boolean hasNext()
  {
    return false;
  }

  public void remove()
  {
  }
}
```

Now client code can treat vice president leaves the same as division branches — even to the extent of getting an iterator for a VP leaf to "iterate" over it. In reality, the vice president leaf iterator only returns the vice president, but now that you have an iterator for each leaf, you don't have to modify code that works with divisions to work with leaves as well.

Creating the division branches

Each branch in the corporate tree is a division of the company which can contain multiple vice presidents — and subdivisions as well. To handle divisions, you decide to modify your `Division` class from earlier in this chapter to make it extend the `Corporate` class, just as the `VP` class did, as shown in the following code:

```
import java.util.*;

public class Division extends Corporate
{
          .
          .
          .
}
```

The rest of the `Division` class is the same as earlier in this chapter, except that you have to convert all its code to deal with `Corporate` objects through composition instead of the `VP` objects you used earlier. Before, the `Division` class stored only VPs because you were dealing with only one division of the company. Now that you're dealing with the whole company, a division can contain subdivisions as well as VPs. Since both divisions and VPs extend the `Corporate` class, you can simply switch to storing and working with `Corporate` objects in the `Division` class — note that the `print` method iterates over all objects in the division, whether they're VPs or divisions.

```
import java.util.*;

public class Division extends Corporate
{
  private Corporate[] corporate = new Corporate[100];
  private int number = 0;
  private String name;

  public Division(String n)
  {
    name = n;
  }
```

```java
public String getName()
{
  return name;
}

public void add(Corporate c)
{
  corporate[number++] = c;
}

public Iterator iterator()
{
  return new DivisionIterator(corporate);
}

public void print()
{
  Iterator iterator = iterator();

  while (iterator.hasNext()){
    Corporate c = (Corporate) iterator.next();
    c.print();
  }
}
}
```

By converting from handling the VP class inside a division to handling the
Corporate class, you can now store VPs or other divisions — and so you're
implementing the Composite design pattern, which says you should be able
to treat leaves or branches as equally as possible.

The division iterator, as implemented by the DivisionIterator class,
is also as it was when you were dealing with a single division that iterated
over the contained vice presidents — except that you also have to switch
DivisionIterator to iterate over Corporate objects (for example, VPs
and other divisions). That looks like this:

```java
import java.util.Iterator;

public class DivisionIterator implements Iterator
{
  private Corporate[] corporate;
  private int location = 0;

  public DivisionIterator(Corporate[] c)
  {
    corporate = c;
  }
```

```
public Corporate next()
{
  return corporate[location++];
}

public boolean hasNext()
{
  if(location < corporate.length && corporate[location] != null){
    return true;
  } else {
    return false;
  }
}

public void remove()
{
}
}
```

You sit back with a satisfied smile, thanks to the Composite pattern. To make the transition from the single-division example in the first half of this chapter to the more involved, tree-like structure of the full corporation example, all you have to do is make sure that all objects in the tree are based on the same class and implement the same methods, allowing them to be treated in the same way.

It's easy to create an overly complex tree structure where you have to treat leaves and branches in entirely separate ways. But it usually makes much more sense to make handling leaves and branches in the same way, and it's not much harder to do that — just make sure you base all tree objects on the same abstract class or interface and implement the same set of methods.

Building your corporation

You've got the vice presidents; you've got the divisions. Now it's time to build the corporation that contains them. To keep this relatively simple, you might just use an `ArrayList` to hold the divisions and vice presidents in the corporation. All the objects in the corporation are `Corporate` objects, so the `ArrayList` will hold `Corporate` objects.

```
import java.util.*;

public class Corporation extends Corporate
{
  private ArrayList<Corporate> corporate = new ArrayList<Corporate>();

  public Corporation()
```

```
    {
    }
       .
       .
       .
}
```

When you want to add a new `Corporate` object to the tree, just use the corporation's `add` method, which just adds the new object to the internal `ArrayList`.

```java
import java.util.*;

public class Corporation extends Corporate
{
  private ArrayList<Corporate> corporate = new ArrayList<Corporate>();

  public Corporation()
  {
  }

  public void add(Corporate c)
  {
    corporate.add(c);
  }
    .
    .
    .
}
```

Want to print out all the objects in the corporation? Just call the corporation's `print` method, which uses the `ArrayList`'s own iterator to print the divisions and vice presidents stored in the corporation — note that when you call a division's `print` method, it iterates over all its internal objects and calls each of their `print` methods. So calling this single `print` method at the `Corporation` level prints out everyone in the corporation.

```java
import java.util.*;

public class Corporation extends Corporate
{
  private ArrayList<Corporate> corporate = new ArrayList<Corporate>();

  public Corporation()
  {
  }

  public void add(Corporate c)
  {
    corporate.add(c);
  }
```

```
  public void print()
  {
    Iterator iterator = corporate.iterator();

    while (iterator.hasNext()){
      Corporate c = (Corporate) iterator.next();
      c.print();
    }
  }
}
```

Time to test it out using the test harness, which is `TestCorporation.java`. You create a new `Corporation` object first.

```
import java.util.*;

public class TestCorporation
{
  Corporation corporation;

  public static void main(String args[])
  {
    TestCorporation t = new TestCorporation();
  }

  public TestCorporation()
  {
    corporation = new Corporation();
    .
    .
    .
}
```

Then you create the R&D division and stock it with vice presidents.

```
import java.util.*;

public class TestCorporation
{
    .
    .
    .
  public TestCorporation()
  {
    corporation = new Corporation();

    Division rnd = new Division("R&D");
    rnd.add(new VP("Steve", "R&D"));
    rnd.add(new VP("Mike", "R&D"));
```

```
        rnd.add(new VP("Nancy", "R&D"));
               .
               .
               .
   }
}
```

Next comes the Sales division. You use the `add` method to add not only vice presidents to this division but also a subdivision, Western Sales, which has its own vice presidents.

```
import java.util.*;

public class TestCorporation
{
      .
      .
      .
   public TestCorporation()
   {
     corporation = new Corporation();

     Division rnd = new Division("R&D");
     rnd.add(new VP("Steve", "R&D"));
     rnd.add(new VP("Mike", "R&D"));
     rnd.add(new VP("Nancy", "R&D"));

     Division sales = new Division("Sales");

     sales.add(new VP("Ted", "Sales"));
     sales.add(new VP("Bob", "Sales"));
     sales.add(new VP("Carol", "Sales"));
     sales.add(new VP("Alice", "Sales"));

     Division western = new Division("Western Sales");
     western.add(new VP("Wally", "Western Sales"));
     western.add(new VP("Andre", "Western Sales"));

     sales.add(western);
           .
           .
           .
   }
}
```

And you can add vice presidents to the corporation directly, as well as divisions, because you can treat leaves and branches equally. After creating a vice president, you can add the vice president — and the divisions you've already created — to the corporation and print the whole thing out with a single call to the corporation's `print` method, which calls the `print` method of each contained object.

```java
import java.util.*;

public class TestCorporation
{
    .
    .
    .
    public TestCorporation()
    {
        corporation = new Corporation();

        Division rnd = new Division("R&D");
        rnd.add(new VP("Steve", "R&D"));
        rnd.add(new VP("Mike", "R&D"));
        rnd.add(new VP("Nancy", "R&D"));

        Division sales = new Division("Sales");

        sales.add(new VP("Ted", "Sales"));
        sales.add(new VP("Bob", "Sales"));
        sales.add(new VP("Carol", "Sales"));
        sales.add(new VP("Alice", "Sales"));

        Division western = new Division("Western Sales");
        western.add(new VP("Wally", "Western Sales"));
        western.add(new VP("Andre", "Western Sales"));

        sales.add(western);

        VP vp = new VP("Cary", "At Large");

        corporation.add(rnd);
        corporation.add(sales);
        corporation.add(vp);

        corporation.print();
    }
}
```

Running the test harness prints out, as it should, the entire corporation's vice presidents.

```
Name: Steve Division: R&D
Name: Mike Division: R&D
Name: Nancy Division: R&D
```

```
Name: Ted Division: Sales
Name: Bob Division: Sales
Name: Carol Division: Sales
Name: Alice Division: Sales
Name: Wally Division: Western Sales
Name: Andre Division: Western Sales
Name: Cary Division: At Large
```

You hand the list triumphantly to the CEO. "Time to start trimming the tree," you say.

"Eh?" asks the CEO.

"Get rid of the deadwood," you say. The CEO hurries off happily.

Tracking the Composite Pattern in the Wild

Are there any examples of the Composite pattern to be found already built into Java, where you can construct trees and treat leaves and branches in much the same way? Sure, there are a few, such as the Node interface you use when you parse XML documents.

In Java, XML nodes can be of several different types as follows:

- ✔ *Document nodes* contain entire XML documents of other nodes.

- ✔ *Text nodes* contain the text in an XML element.

- ✔ *XML processing instructions.*

- ✔ *XML elements* can contain child elements, which themselves can contain child elements, and so on.

But all these node types have one thing in common — they all implement the Node interface. XML documents are parsed into trees of nodes, and because all the nodes implement the Node interface, you can handle them in the same way. There's an example in the code for this book, Parser.java, as well as a sample XML file you can run it on, sample.xml. The Parser application uses a Java DocumentBuilder object to parse XML files you pass to it on the command line (run it like this: java Parser sample.xml), which creates a tree of nodes. The Parser application walks that tree and prints out the XML document properly indented.

Because you can handle all the nodes in the tree in essentially the same way, `Parser.java` only needs one recursive method (that is, this method calls itself), `display`, to walk through the entire tree. The `display` method takes two arguments — the current node in the tree, and the current `indentation` string. Because each object in the tree implements the `Node` interface, it doesn't matter what kind of node you call the `display` method with — an element node, a processing instruction node, whatever. If the current node has children, the `display` method iterates over them recursively as well. To walk the entire tree, all you have to do is pass this method the document node you get when you parse the XML document with `DocumentBuilder`, and it works from node to node from then on. Here's what the `display` method looks like:

```java
public void display(Node node, String indentation)
{
    if (node == null) {
        return;
    }

    int type = node.getNodeType();

    switch (type) {
        case Node.DOCUMENT_NODE: {
            text[numberOfLines] = indentation;
            text[numberOfLines] += "<?xml version=\"1.0\" encoding=\"" +
              "UTF-8" + "\"?>";
            numberOfLines++;
            display(((Document)node).getDocumentElement(), "");
            break;
        }

        case Node.ELEMENT_NODE: {

            text[numberOfLines] = indentation;
            text[numberOfLines] += "<";
            text[numberOfLines] += node.getNodeName();

            int length = (node.getAttributes() != null) ?
              node.getAttributes().getLength() : 0;
            Attr attributes[] = new Attr[length];
            for (int loopIndex = 0; loopIndex < length; loopIndex++) {
                attributes[loopIndex] =
                  (Attr)node.getAttributes().item(loopIndex);
            }

            for (int loopIndex = 0; loopIndex < attributes.length;
              loopIndex++) {
                Attr attribute = attributes[loopIndex];
                text[numberOfLines] += " ";
```

```
                    text[numberOfLines] += attribute.getNodeName();
                    text[numberOfLines] += "=\"";
                    text[numberOfLines] += attribute.getNodeValue();
                    text[numberOfLines] += "\"";
                }
                text[numberOfLines]+=">";

                numberOfLines++;

                NodeList childNodes = node.getChildNodes();
                if (childNodes != null) {
                    length = childNodes.getLength();
                    indentation += "    ";
                    for (int loopIndex = 0; loopIndex < length; loopIndex++ ) {
                        display(childNodes.item(loopIndex), indentation);
                    }
                }
                break;
            }

            case Node.CDATA_SECTION_NODE: {
                text[numberOfLines] = indentation;
                text[numberOfLines] += "<![CDATA[";
                text[numberOfLines] += node.getNodeValue();
                text[numberOfLines] += "]]>";
                numberOfLines++;
                break;
            }

            case Node.TEXT_NODE: {
                text[numberOfLines] = indentation;
                String newText = node.getNodeValue().trim();
                if(newText.indexOf("\n") < 0 && newText.length() > 0) {
                    text[numberOfLines] += newText;
                    numberOfLines++;
                }
                break;
            }

            case Node.PROCESSING_INSTRUCTION_NODE: {
                text[numberOfLines] = indentation;
                text[numberOfLines] += "<?";
                text[numberOfLines] += node.getNodeName();
                String value = node.getNodeValue();
                if (value != null && value.length() > 0) {
                    text[numberOfLines] += value;
                }
                text[numberOfLines] += "?>";
                numberOfLines++;
                break;
```

```
            }
        }

    if (type == Node.ELEMENT_NODE) {
        text[numberOfLines] = indentation.substring(0, indentation.length()
            - 4);
        text[numberOfLines] += "</";
        text[numberOfLines] += node.getNodeName();
        text[numberOfLines] += ">";
        numberOfLines++;
        indentation += "    ";
    }
}
```

That's how it works — when you parse an XML document in Java, you get a tree of nodes where each node, whether it's the tree or a branch, implements the Node interface. And for that reason, you can handle trees and branches in the same way in your code. Cool. That's the Composite pattern at work.

Chapter 9

Getting Control of Your Objects with the State and Proxy Patterns

The CEO of Apartments-N-Stuff Inc. has reserved your services as a consultant and says, "We run huge, apartment-rental complexes all around the country. Our big problem is property managers — they cost too much. So we're going to convert all our apartment complexes to use rental automats — robots that will accept rental applications and dispense keys — instead. We want new tenants to be able to submit their rental applications to an automat and, if they're approved, get their keys from that automat."

"Sounds nuts," you say.

"Here's the idea," says the CEO. "Normally, the automat just sits around waiting for a prospective tenant to show up. When a tenant does submit an application, the automat checks it. If the application is approved, the automat should dispense keys to the tenant; otherwise, the automat should tell the tenant he was rejected and go back to waiting. Oh, and if the automat rents out an apartment, the automat should check if there are still any apartments left in the complex and not rent any more if there aren't."

The CEO watches as you scribble on a pad of paper and finally asks, "What are you doing?"

"I'm drawing a state diagram," you say.

"Can I see it?" asks the CEO.

"No," you say. "You would need a great deal more intelligence to understand this."

"Oh," says the CEO.

This chapter is about two patterns: the State pattern, where an object keeps track of its internal state, and can change its behavior based on that state, and the Proxy pattern, where one object can act as a substitute for another. You're going to see how both work in detail in this chapter.

Getting the State of Your Union with the State Pattern

You understand what the CEO told you. The rental automat has the following four *states* (as in, "conditions of being," not political states or areas on a map):

✓ Waiting for a new tenant
✓ Receiving an application
✓ Renting an apartment
✓ Fully rented

Figure 9-1 shows your state diagram, where each box represents a different state of being, and you've connected the states to make a representation of the automat:

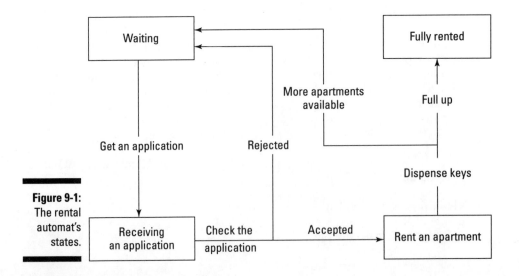

Figure 9-1: The rental automat's states.

This, you think to yourself, is a job for the State design pattern.

Sometimes, when you're engaged on a larger project, the coding starts to feel very murky. There are just so many possible conditions that you have to deal with that it's tough to know where the boundaries are or how to divide your code.

When you face a large-scale application and the coding gets out of hand, it often helps to start thinking in terms of various states. This device helps you segment your code into independent units (states) — ideally, each state should be logically independent of the others, so thinking in terms of states can automatically divide your code into discrete sections.

The Gang of Four (GoF) book *(Design Patterns: Elements of Reusable Object-Oriented Software, 1995, Pearson Education, Inc. Publishing as Pearson Addison Wesley)* says that the State design pattern will "Allow an object to alter its behavior when its internal state changes. The object will appear to change its class."

In other words, your code should keep track of an internal state, such as the `Waiting for a new tenant` state. Any part of the code can check what the current state is and react accordingly. For example, if the rental automat is in the `Fully rented` state and a prospective new tenant gives it a rental application, it should reject that application.

When you use the State pattern, any part of your code can check what state is current. That can clarify and centralize the workings of very large pieces of code because you have control over what far-flung code segments do, just by changing the current state.

In general, the State pattern is useful when you've got a lot of code that's getting more and more murky and complex. If you can compartmentalize the working of what you're trying to do into a set of independent states, you can compartmentalize your code.

Using methods to hold state

Here's a first, simple attempt at coding the rental automat, using states. You decide that you might be able to write the application centered on a set of methods which do different things depending on the current state. Here's what it looks like in `RentalMethods.java` — you start by creating a constant for each of the four possible states of the rental automat, as well as an internal variable named `state` that holds the current state (which is set to `WAITING`, when the application starts):

```
import java.util.*;
import java.lang.Math;

public class RentalMethods
```

```
{
  final static int FULLY_RENTED = 0;
  final static int WAITING = 1;
  final static int GOT_APPLICATION = 2;
  final static int APARTMENT_RENTED = 3;
  int state = WAITING;
    .
    .
    .
```

Now any code in the application can check the current state and respond accordingly. For example, the following code shows how the getApplication method works, which is called when the automat gets a prospective tenant application — note how what happens depends on the internal state:

```
import java.util.*;
import java.lang.Math;

public class RentalMethods
{
  final static int FULLY_RENTED = 0;
  final static int WAITING = 1;
  final static int GOT_APPLICATION = 2;
  final static int APARTMENT_RENTED = 3;
  Random random;
  int numberApartments;
  int state = WAITING;

  public RentalMethods(int n)
  {
    numberApartments = n;
    random = new Random(System.currentTimeMillis());
  }

  public void getApplication()
  {
    switch (state)
    {
      case FULLY_RENTED:
        System.out.println("Sorry, we're fully rented.");
        break;
      case WAITING:
        state = GOT_APPLICATION;
        System.out.println("Thanks for the application.");
        break;
      case GOT_APPLICATION:
        System.out.println("We already got your application.");
        break;
      case APARTMENT_RENTED:
        System.out.println("Hang on, we're renting you an apartment.");
```

```
        break;
    }
}
    .
    .
    .
```

So if the automat gets an application and it's in the FULLY_RENTED state, the automat prints out Sorry, we're fully rented. If the automat gets an application and it's in the WAITING state, on the other hand, it displays Thanks for the application. and changes the internal state to GOT_APPLICATION.

Similarly, if you call the automat's checkApplication method, the response depends on the current state: For example, if the automat is asked to check an application and it's in the WAITING state, it tells the prospective tenant she has to submit an application first. If the automat is in the GOT_ APPLICATION state when you call its checkApplication method, it should check that application and either accept or reject the tenant. That process is simulated in this example with a random number — if the application is accepted, the code puts the automat in the APARTMENT_RENTED state and calls a method named rentApartment; if the application is rejected, the code puts the automat into the WAITING state.

```
public void checkApplication()
{
    int yesno = random.nextInt() % 10;

    switch (state)
    {
      case FULLY_RENTED:
        System.out.println("Sorry, we're fully rented.");
        break;
      case WAITING:
        System.out.println("You have to submit an application.");
        break;
      case GOT_APPLICATION:
        if (yesno > 4 && numberApartments > 0) {
          System.out.println("Congratulations, you were approved.");
          state = APARTMENT_RENTED;
          rentApartment();
        } else {
          System.out.println("Sorry, you were not approved.");
          state = WAITING;
        }
        break;
      case APARTMENT_RENTED:
        System.out.println("Hang on, we're renting you an apartment.");
        break;
    }
}
```

The rentApartment method also checks the internal state — if that state is APARTMENT_RENTED, it decrements the number of available apartments by 1 and calls the dispenseKeys method.

```
public void rentApartment()
{
  switch (state)
  {
    case FULLY_RENTED:
      System.out.println("Sorry, we're fully rented.");
      break;
    case WAITING:
      System.out.println("You have to submit an application.");
      break;
    case GOT_APPLICATION:
      System.out.println("You must have your application checked.");
      break;
    case APARTMENT_RENTED:
      System.out.println("Renting you an apartment....");
      numberApartments--;
      dispenseKeys();
      break;
  }
}
```

Finally, the dispenseKeys method also checks the current state and, if that state is APARTMENT_RENTED, gives the keys to the new tenant and then puts the automat into the WATING state for the next prospective tenant.

```
public void dispenseKeys()
{
  switch (state)
  {
    case FULLY_RENTED:
      System.out.println("Sorry, we're fully rented.");
      break;
    case WAITING:
      System.out.println("You have to submit an application.");
      break;
    case GOT_APPLICATION:
      System.out.println("You must have your application checked.");
      break;
    case APARTMENT_RENTED:
      System.out.println("Here are your keys!");
      state = WAITING;
      break;
  }
}
```

That's the idea — you keep track of the internal state and every time external code calls one of your `public` methods, you can check that current state to see what to do. Here's a test harness for the `RentalMethods` class you just developed, `TestRentalMethods.java`. This test harness creates a new `RentalMethods` object, passing the constructor a value of 9 to indicate that there are nine apartments for rent. Then the code calls the `getApplication` and `checkApplication` methods to mimic a new tenant.

```
public class TestRentalMethods
{
  RentalMethods rentalMethods;

  public static void main(String args[])
  {
    TestRentalMethods t = new TestRentalMethods();
  }

  public TestRentalMethods()
  {
    rentalMethods = new RentalMethods(9);

    rentalMethods.getApplication();
    rentalMethods.checkApplication();

  }
}
```

And here's the result:

```
Thanks for the application.
Congratulations, you were approved.
Renting you an apartment....
Here are your keys!
```

Not bad — you were able to implement the rental automat.

But there's a problem with this method-based approach. As you add more states, each method becomes longer and longer, and each method has to be rewritten for all the new states. What should you do? When in doubt, encapsulate.

Using objects to encapsulate state

Instead of giving each state its own constant, it's a better idea to give each state its own *class*. That way, you can call methods like `dispenseKeys` or `checkApplication` on a `state` object anywhere in your code. All you have to do is load the correct `state` object into a generic variable and call various methods of that variable. For example, if the current `state` object corresponds to a waiting state, you're going to get a very different response when you call its `gotApplication` method than if the current `state` object corresponds to a fully rented state, where no more apartments are available.

You decide to try holding the current state in an object to make your code cleaner. How would you design the automat to use such `state` objects? The automat stores the current state in a `state` object, which can hold any of the four possible `state` objects: `WaitingState`, `GotApplicationState`, `ApartmentRentedState`, and `FullyRentedState` (see Figure 9-2).

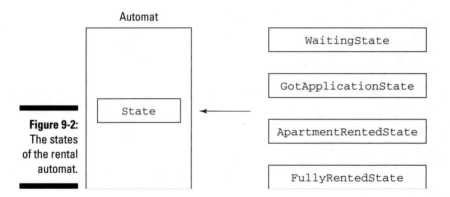

Figure 9-2:
The states of the rental automat.

The automat code can then simply work with the current `state` object, calling that object's methods, such as `checkApplication` — depending on what the current state is, you get an appropriate response from the `state` object.

You start putting the automat together, beginning with an interface that lists the methods the automat should support. The automat should be able to interact with the user with the same methods you've already seen — `checkApplication`, `rentApartment`, and so on, so you add those methods first, as shown in the following:

```
public interface AutomatInterface
{
    public void gotApplication();
    public void checkApplication();
    public void rentApartment();
        .
        .
        .
}
```

While it's doing its work, a particular state object might decide that it's time for the automat to change state. For example, if the current state is represented by a WaitingState object and you tell it that you got a rental application, that object might want to change the current state to a GotApplicationState object. To allow state objects to change the state stored in the automat, the automat should support a setState method. And you can also add methods to create the new state objects, which can be called as needed.

```
public interface AutomatInterface
{
    public void gotApplication();
    public void checkApplication();
    public void rentApartment();
    public void setState(State s);
    public State getWaitingState();
    public State getGotApplicationState();
    public State getApartmentRentedState();
    public State getFullyRentedState();



        .

        .

        .

}
```

Finally, the state objects need to know how many apartments are available to rent (to check if the automat should go to a FullyRentedState state or not after an apartment is rented), so you might add a getCount and setCount method that gets and sets the current number of apartments for rent.

```
public interface AutomatInterface
{
    public void gotApplication();
    public void checkApplication();
    public void rentApartment();
    public void setState(State s);
    public State getWaitingState();
    public State getGotApplicationState();
    public State getApartmentRentedState();
    public State getFullyRentedState();
    public int getCount();
    public void setCount(int n);
}
```

Those are the methods the automat supports; now it's time to create the automat itself. You start the Automat class by implementing this new interface, AutomatInterface.

```
public class Automat implements AutomatInterface
{



        .

        .

        .

}
```

You pass the number of apartments available for rent to the automat constructor. The constructor also creates four state objects corresponding to the four possible states — WaitingState, GotApplicationState, ApartmentRentedState, and FullyRentedState — so it can switch between those states as needed. The automat's current state is stored in a variable named state, and the constructor sets that to a WaitingState object initially.

```
public class Automat implements AutomatInterface
{
  State waitingState;
  State gotApplicationState;
  State apartmentRentedState;
  State fullyRentedState;
  State state;
  int count;

  public Automat(int n)
  {
    count = n;
    waitingState = new WaitingState(this);
    gotApplicationState = new GotApplicationState(this);
    apartmentRentedState = new ApartmentRentedState(this);
    waitingState = new WaitingState(this);
    state = waitingState;
  }
      .
      .
      .
}
```

Now you can add methods like gotApplication to the automat so that it can interact with a prospective tenant. For example, when the automat gets an application, all it has to do is call the current state object's got Application method, and that method returns text which the automat can display. Here's how you implement the methods like gotApplication and checkApplication that let the automat interact with a prospective tenant — note that all you have to do is call methods of the current state object, simple as pie:

```
public class Automat implements AutomatInterface
{
  State waitingState;
  State gotApplicationState;
  State apartmentRentedState;
  State fullyRentedState;
  State state;
  int count;
```

```
public Automat(int n)
{
  count = n;
  waitingState = new WaitingState(this);
  gotApplicationState = new GotApplicationState(this);
  apartmentRentedState = new ApartmentRentedState(this);
  waitingState = new WaitingState(this);
  state = waitingState;
}

public void gotApplication()
{
  System.out.println(state.gotApplication());
}

public void checkApplication()
{
  System.out.println(state.checkApplication());
}

public void rentApartment()
{
  System.out.println(state.rentApartment());
  System.out.println(state.dispenseKeys());
}
    .
    .
    .
}
```

All that's left to do now is implement the utility methods that return new
`state` objects as needed, set the state as needed, and get or set the count
of available apartments, as shown here:

```
public class Automat implements AutomatInterface
{
  State waitingState;
  State gotApplicationState;
  State apartmentRentedState;
  State fullyRentedState;
  State state;
  int count;
      .
      .
      .

  public State getApartmentRentedState()
  {
    return apartmentRentedState;
  }
```

```
public State getFullyRentedState()
{
  return fullyRentedState;
}

public int getCount()
{
  return count;
}

public void setCount(int n)
{
  count = n;
}

public void setState(State s)
{
  state = s;
}
```

That completes the `Automat` class. You've offloaded most of the work to `state` objects, and now it's time to create those objects.

Creating the state objects

Each `state` object supports the methods `gotApplication`, `check Application`, `rentApplication`, and `dispenseKeys`, but of course, each `state` object handles those methods in a different way. If you try to call `dispenseKeys` when the automat is in the fully rented state, for example, you're not going to get any keys. To make sure each `state` object implements all the methods it should, you create an interface named `State`.

```
public interface State
{
  public String gotApplication();
  public String checkApplication();
  public String rentApartment();
  public String dispenseKeys();
}
```

The `WaitingState` class corresponds to the waiting state, and because it's a `state` class, it implements the `State` interface.

```
public class WaitingState implements State
{
     .
     .
     .
}
```

The `automat` object is passed to each `state` object's constructor, so the code in `WaitingState` starts by storing the `automat` object.

```
public class WaitingState implements State
{
  AutomatInterface automat;

  public WaitingState(AutomatInterface a)
  {
    automat = a;
  }
      .
      .
      .
}
```

If the automat is in the waiting state and gets an application, the automat should switch to the `GotApplicationState` state and return an acknowledgement that it received that application. Here's what that looks like in the `WaitingState` class's `gotApplication` method:

```
public class WaitingState implements State
{
  AutomatInterface automat;

  public WaitingState(AutomatInterface a)
  {
    automat = a;
  }

  public String gotApplication()
  {
    automat.setState(automat.getGotApplicationState());
    return "Thanks for the application.";
  }
      .
      .
      .
}
```

Now you've delegated what happens to the `state` objects and even let them switch the automat's state as needed. Here are the other methods of the `WaitingState` class:

```
public class WaitingState implements State
{
  AutomatInterface automat;

  public WaitingState(AutomatInterface a)
  {
    automat = a;
  }
```

```
  public String gotApplication()
  {
    automat.setState(automat.getGotApplicationState());
    return "Thanks for the application.";
  }

  public String checkApplication()
  {
    return "You have to submit an application.";
  }

  public String rentApartment()
  {
    return "You have to submit an application.";
  }

  public String dispenseKeys()
  {
    return "You have to submit an application.";
  }
}
```

The GotApplicationState class handles the state where the automat
gets an application. The big method here is checkApplication, which
accepts or rejects the application and changes the automat's state to match
(to the ApartmentRentedState if the application is accepted, or to the
WaitingState if it's not).

```
import java.util.*;
import java.lang.Math;

public class GotApplicationState implements State
{
  AutomatInterface automat;
  Random random;

  public GotApplicationState(AutomatInterface a)
  {
    automat = a;
    random = new Random(System.currentTimeMillis());
  }

  public String gotApplication()
  {
    return "We already got your application.";
  }

  public String checkApplication()
  {
```

```
    int yesno = random.nextInt() % 10;

    if (yesno > 4 && automat.getCount() > 0) {
      automat.setState(automat.getApartmentRentedState());
      return "Congratulations, you were approved.";
    } else {
      automat.setState(automat.getWaitingState());
      return "Sorry, you were not approved.";
    }
  }

  public String rentApartment()
  {
    return "You must have your application checked.";
  }

  public String dispenseKeys()
  {
    return "You must have your application checked.";
  }
}
```

If the prospective renter's application is accepted, the automat's internal state is set to an ApartmentRentedState object. This state object has two important methods: rentApartment and dispenseKeys. The dispenseKeys method is the final step of the whole automat process; if there are more apartments to rent, the automat goes back to the waiting state, but if there are no more apartments to rent, it goes to the fully rented state.

```
public class ApartmentRentedState implements State
{
  AutomatInterface automat;

  public ApartmentRentedState(AutomatInterface a)
  {
    automat = a;
  }

  public String gotApplication()
  {
    return "Hang on, we're renting you an apartment.";
  }

  public String checkApplication()
  {
    return "Hang on, we're renting you an apartment.";
  }
```

```
public String rentApartment()
{
  automat.setCount(automat.getCount() - 1);
  return "Renting you an apartment....";
}

public String dispenseKeys()
{
  if(automat.getCount() <= 0){
    automat.setState(automat.getFullyRentedState());
  } else {
    automat.setState(automat.getWaitingState());
  }
  return "Here are your keys!";
}
}
```

The fully rented state is easy to code — the automat has nothing to rent, so this state just blocks all actions and returns the message Sorry, we're fully rented.

```
public class FullyRentedState implements State
{
  AutomatInterface automat;

  public FullyRentedState(AutomatInterface a)
  {
    automat = a;
  }

  public String gotApplication()
  {
    return "Sorry, we're fully rented.";
  }

  public String checkApplication()
  {
    return "Sorry, we're fully rented.";
  }

  public String rentApartment()
  {
    return "Sorry, we're fully rented.";
  }

  public String dispenseKeys()
  {
    return "Sorry, we're fully rented.";
  }
}
```

That gives you the Automat class and the four state object classes. Now it's time to give this code a test drive.

Putting the rental automat to the test

A likely looking prospective candidate walks through the door and plunks down a rental application, saying, "How about it?"

Having just finished creating the rental automat, you look up from your keyboard and say, "You're just in time. I'm writing the test harness now." To test the automat — say you've got 9 apartments to rent — you can create an `Automat` object by passing 9 to the `Automat` constructor, then call that object's `gotApplication`, `checkApplication`, and `rentApartment` methods; the automat changes the internal state automatically, as needed. The test harness, `TestAutomat.java`, looks like the following:

```java
public class TestAutomat
{
  Automat automat;

  public static void main(String args[])
  {
    TestAutomat t = new TestAutomat();
  }

  public TestAutomat()
  {
    automat = new Automat(9);

    automat.gotApplication();
    automat.checkApplication();
    automat.rentApartment();
  }
}
```

The result? Does the applicant get an apartment? Take a look for yourself when you run the test harness.

```
Thanks for the application.
Congratulations, you were approved.
Renting you an apartment....
Here are your keys!
```

Beautiful. Note what you've done — you've simplified the code in the automat dramatically by offloading it to `state` objects. The code in the automat doesn't have to change to handle different states; only the `state` object itself changes. And each new `state` object has its own built-in methods to handle any requests made of it, appropriately, for the state it represents. By encapsulating how you handle each state in separate `state` objects, the code is easier to modify and maintain.

Standing In for Other Objects with Proxies

The CEO of Apartments-N-Stuff Inc. is back with congratulations. "Your automat works terrific," the CEO says. "So now we'd like to modify it."

"You haven't paid my bill yet," you point out.

"Here's the idea," the CEO says. "We've installed your automats at all our rental developments throughout the country — and now we're after the international market. Is there some way to let prospective tenants interact with your automat no matter where they are in the world?"

"Sure," you say, "using the Proxy design pattern, you can have a local object that 'stands in' for a remote object. As far as the local code knows, it's dealing with the real thing instead of the proxy."

"Fine," says the CEO. "Get to work."

"Fine," you say, "pay my bill."

Here's the problem though: You've got a client somewhere in the world, and the automat somewhere else, and the two are separate, as shown in Figure 9-3.

Figure 9-3:
Separate
client and
automat.

Client		Automat

And here's how proxies fix the situation: You can give the client code a proxy object that "stands in" or substitutes for the automat object and looks just like it as far as the programming goes (that is, it supports the same methods). The proxy can communicate with the remote automat code in an automat server, as shown in Figure 9-4.

Figure 9-4:
A proxy
acting like
an automat.

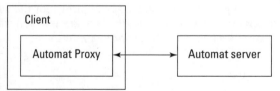

To the client code, which is working with the automat proxy, it feels just as though it's working with an automat object directly. In fact, the automat proxy is just there to communicate with the automat server, which does the real work of the automat and communicates with the proxy.

The GoF book says you can use the Proxy design pattern to, "Provide a surrogate or placeholder for another object to control access to it."

The Proxy design pattern is your best friend when you have a remote object you want to work with and make that object seem local, or when you want to control access to that remote object in some way.

The Proxy pattern is easy enough to put to work. After accepting your fat fee from the CEO of Apartments-N-Stuff Inc., you set to work. The CEO wants the automat proxy to be able to connect to an automat server anywhere in the world, so you decide to use the Internet. There are various connection techniques you can use in Java, such as RMI, to enable proxies to talk to remote objects. Since all you have to do is send text back and forth from automat proxy to automat server, you decide that it's simpler to go with Java sockets and text streams.

The code you're about to develop can send text back and forth between any two points on the Internet — if you want to, it's easily adaptable to create your own messaging service or private e-mail system. All you need to do is make sure the server has a fixed IP address — and if you have broadband, you should.

Can you hear me now? Creating the automat server

You set to work on the automat server first. This is just an automat that can talk to an automat proxy over the Internet. For example, the proxy can send text messages like `"checkApplication"` or `"rentApartment"` to the automat server, and the server can call those methods and send back the response to the proxy.

So how do you set up an automat so it can talk to an automat proxy over the Internet? All you need to do is use a Java `ServerSocket` and set up an `InputStream` and an `OutputStream` to communicate with the automat proxy. You can make life easy on yourself by using the `OutputStream` to create a `PrintWriter` object that lets you use the `println` method to send text back to the proxy. And the `InputStream` has to handle text whenever it comes in from the proxy, so you can handle that in a new thread.

The server can be configured to listen for connections on port 8765 — that's just a random port; if you want to use a different port, just change that value in the code. The following code shows how to set up the PrintWriter for outgoing text and the thread to handle the incoming text in the Automat Server class's constructor:

```
import java.io.*;
import java.net.*;

public class AutomatServer implements Runable, AutomatInterface
{
  State waitingState;
  State gotApplicationState;
  State apartmentRentedState;
  State fullyRentedState;
  State state;
  int count;
  private Thread thread;
  ServerSocket socket;
  PrintWriter out;
  Socket communicationSocket;

  public static void main(String args[])
  {
    AutomatServer d = new AutomatServer();
  }

  public AutomatServer()
  {
    count = 9;
    waitingState = new WaitingState(this);
    gotApplicationState = new GotApplicationState(this);
    apartmentRentedState = new ApartmentRentedState(this);
    waitingState = new WaitingState(this);
    state = waitingState;

    try {
      socket = new ServerSocket(8765);

      communicationSocket = socket.accept();

      out = new PrintWriter (communicationSocket.getOutputStream(), true);

      thread = new Thread(this);
      thread.start();

    }
    catch (Exception e)
    {
```

```
        System.err.println(e.getMessage());
    }
}
        .
        .
        .
```

The next step is to set up an InputStream to handle text sent from the proxy
in the worker thread's run method. You can make life easier here, too, by
using that InputStream to create a BufferedReader object that lets you
read incoming text, line by line, with its readLine method. The messages
sent from the proxy can be "checkApplication" or "rentApartment",
and so on, and you should call the appropriate Automat methods to match.
Here's how the automat server waits for messages from the proxy and calls
the correct local Automat methods as needed:

```
public void run()
{
  String incomingString;
  try {

    BufferedReader in = new BufferedReader (new
    InputStreamReader(communicationSocket.getInputStream()));
    while((incomingString = in.readLine()) != null){
      if (incomingString.equals("gotApplication")){
        gotApplication();
      } else if (incomingString.equals("checkApplication")) {
        checkApplication();
      } else if (incomingString.equals("rentApartment")) {
        rentApartment();
      }
    }
  }catch (Exception e)
  {
    System.err.println(e.getMessage());
  }
}
```

Before using a proxy, the Automat methods like checkApplication and
rentApartment used to display text returned from the current state
object this way:

```
public void gotApplication()
{
  System.out.println(state.gotApplication());
}

public void checkApplication()
```

```
  {
    System.out.println(state.checkApplication());
  }

  public void rentApartment()
  {
    System.out.println(state.rentApartment());
    System.out.println(state.dispenseKeys());
  }
```

But that's not going to work here — you have to use the `PrintWriter` object, `out`, to send text back to the proxy. Here's what the `Automat` methods look like as adapted for the automat server, sending text back to the proxy as appropriate:

```
public void gotApplication()
{
  out.println(state.gotApplication());
}

public void checkApplication()
{
  out.println(state.checkApplication());
}

public void rentApartment()
{
  out.println(state.rentApartment());
  out.println(state.dispenseKeys());
}
```

That completes the automat server. When the automat proxy connects to it, it can accept commands and send the results back. How about creating the proxy?

Anyone there? Creating the automat proxy

The automat proxy's job is to connect to the automat server across the Internet while letting the client code think that it's interacting with a standard, local automat. The automat server has to be running and listening on its machine before the automat proxy can connect to it. Here's how the connection process works — you pass the IP address and port number to the `Socket` constructor. In this example, the IP address is 127.0.0.1, which stands for the same machine you're executing the code on. (So to make this work in Windows, for example, open a second DOS window and start the automat server there before starting the test harness.) If you want to connect across the Internet to another machine, just replace the IP address with the IP address of the machine where the automat server is running. The following code shows how the automat proxy sets up the connection to the server, creating objects named `in` and `out` to receive and send data:

```java
import java.io.*;
import java.net.*;

public class AutomatProxy implements Runable
{
  private Thread thread;
  Socket socket;
  InputStream in;
  PrintWriter out;
  int character;

  public AutomatProxy()
  {
    try{
      socket = new Socket("127.0.0.1", 8765);
      System.out.println("Connecting....");

      in = socket.getInputStream();
      out = new PrintWriter (socket.getOutputStream(), true);

      thread = new Thread(this);
      thread.start();
    }
    catch (IOException ioe){
      System.err.println("The server must be running.");
      System.err.println("Not connected");
    }
    catch (Exception e){
      System.err.println(e.getMessage());
    }

    if(socket != null && socket.isConnected()){
      System.out.println("Connected");
    }
  }
  .
  .
  .
```

When the client code calls the proxy's standard `automat` methods — `got Application`, `checkApplication`, and `rentApartment`, the proxy sends the name of the called method to the automat server using its `PrintWriter` object named `out`.

```
public void gotApplication()
{
  out.println("gotApplication");
}

public void checkApplication()
{
  out.println("checkApplication");
}

public void rentApartment()
{
  out.println("rentApartment");
}
```

That takes care of sending commands to the automat server. What about listening for a response? Like the automat server, the automat proxy launches a new thread to listen with. The following code shows how it listens for text coming back from the server in the thread's `run` method — when text comes back from the server, the proxy prints that text out.

```
public void run()
{
  try{
    while ((character = in.read()) != -1) {
      System.out.print((char) character);
    }
  }
  catch(Exception ex){
    System.out.println(ex.getMessage());
  }
}
```

Now you've built an automat proxy that connects to an automat server and added the code that lets the two communicate. Time to test this out.

Using the proxy to connect around the world

To test the automat proxy and server, start the server (if you're testing this on a single machine in Windows, start the server in a new DOS window) and run the code in the test harness, `TestAutomatProxy.java`. This test harness uses an automat proxy in the same way as it would use an `automat` object. Behind the scenes, the automat proxy connects to the automat server and passes on all it's asked to do to the automat server.

Here's the code that shows how the test harness uses the automat proxy to get an application, check it, and rent an apartment:

```
public class TestAutomatProxy
{
  AutomatProxy automatProxy;

  public static void main(String args[])
  {
    TestAutomatProxy t = new TestAutomatProxy();
  }

  public TestAutomatProxy()
  {
    automatProxy = new AutomatProxy();

    automatProxy.gotApplication();
    automatProxy.checkApplication();
    automatProxy.rentApartment();
  }
}
```

What's the result? First the proxy connects to the server, then it sends the commands the automat server should run, and then it displays the text it gets back. Here's what a prospective tenant in another country sees:

```
Connecting....
Connected
Thanks for the application.
Congratulations, you were approved.
Renting you an apartment....
Here are your keys!
```

"There you go," you say to the CEO of Apartments-N-Stuff Inc. "Now you're renting apartments internationally, over the Internet."

"Yeah," says the CEO thoughtfully. "Maybe we better change that last line to We're *mailing* you the keys. now."

Chapter 10

Coordinating Your Objects with the Command and Mediator Patterns

*Y*ou're consulting for GlobalHugeCo, the computer manufacturer, when the Chief Information Officer comes in, looks at a monitor on the wall, and says, "Uh oh."

"What's the problem?" you ask.

"We run servers for different regions of the world, and it's mission-critical that we keep those servers operating."

"And there's a problem?" you ask.

The CIO looks wearily at the monitor on the wall and says, "We've got a 24-hour Crisis Center that handles calls from our major customers. If there's a problem with the servers, we know about it instantly. However, there's a problem with the Crisis Center."

"And that is?"

"Our software is so confusing that the Crisis Center typically gets all bollixed up before it can handle any problem. If there's a problem with the Asia server, our techs have to connect to the Asia server, run diagnostics, and disconnect again. Meanwhile, a problem with the Euro server might have come up, and they have to connect to the Euro server, reboot it, and disconnect. Then the U.S. server starts acting up again. So they get all confused making dozens of method calls among all the different servers."

"Hmm," you say, "this sounds like a job for the Command design pattern."

"That's just what I said to them," the CIO says.

This chapter is about two related design patterns — the Command and Mediator design patterns, which are all about letting you interact with and coordinate other objects.

The Command design pattern lets you package complex commands into a single object. Rather than having to perform the multiple steps needed to execute each command every time, you can create a bunch of ready-to-use command objects, each of which can handle multiple steps internally. Each command is already configured with its target (such as the Asia server) and the action it's supposed to perform (such as reboot a server), so a set of command objects can act as a ready-made toolkit, already configured and all set to operate on the target objects they're supposed to handle.

The Mediator design pattern also supports coordination between objects. You may have, for example, a dozen different windows in a GUI, all connected in intricate ways. When the user clicks one button in one window (such as the Exit, Purchase Now!, or Shop buttons), a window has to pass control on to another window and let that next window know what the current state is — for example, `"the user wants to make a purchase"`, `"the user wants to exit"`, and so on. The more windows, the more difficult it is to coordinate them all because they're tightly coupled. A mediator makes the coupling looser by having all objects report state changes to the mediator and take commands from the mediator. That way, each window in your GUI only has to interact with the mediator, and doesn't have to understand all the methods to call in the various other windows. This chapter shows you how to simplify your windows with the Mediator design pattern.

Taking Command with the Command Pattern

There you are, the famous and well-paid design pattern consultant, at work on the CIO of GlobalHugeCo's problem. You understand the problem; when a crisis happens in one of the company's three servers, the Crisis Center has to react fast. But the programmers in the Crisis Center only have a bunch of methods ready for use, as illustrated in Figure 10-1.

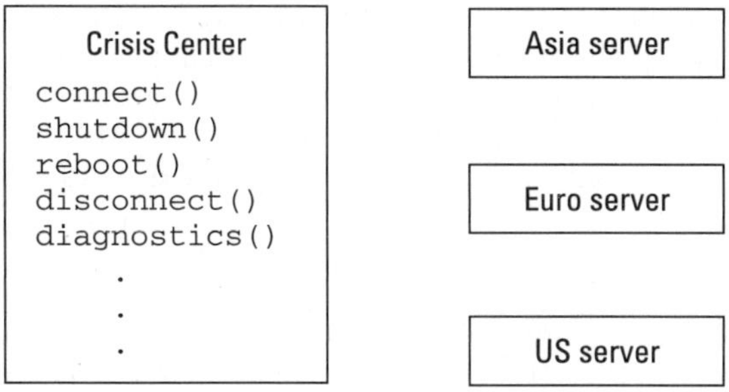

```
┌─────────────────────┐        ┌──────────────────┐
│    Crisis Center     │        │   Asia server    │
│                      │        └──────────────────┘
│  connect()           │
│  shutdown()          │
│  reboot()            │        ┌──────────────────┐
│  disconnect()        │        │   Euro server    │
│  diagnostics()       │        └──────────────────┘
│        .             │
│        .             │        ┌──────────────────┐
│        .             │        │    US server     │
└─────────────────────┘        └──────────────────┘
```

Figure 10-1:
The Crisis
Center and
its methods.

When there's a crisis, the Crisis Center programmers have to call the `connect` method of the correct server, then take actions like shutting down the server or running diagnostics on it, and then have to disconnect from the server. That confuses them — sometimes commands are sent to the wrong server, or programmers forget to connect to a server before issuing commands to it, and so on. But the Command design pattern is here to fix all that.

The Command design pattern says that in cases like this, you should encapsulate all the separate actions into objects configured for specific targets. That gives you a number of objects that act like a set of tools, ready to be used. Figure 10-2 shows what the Crisis Center's toolkit might look like, with ready-to-use command objects.

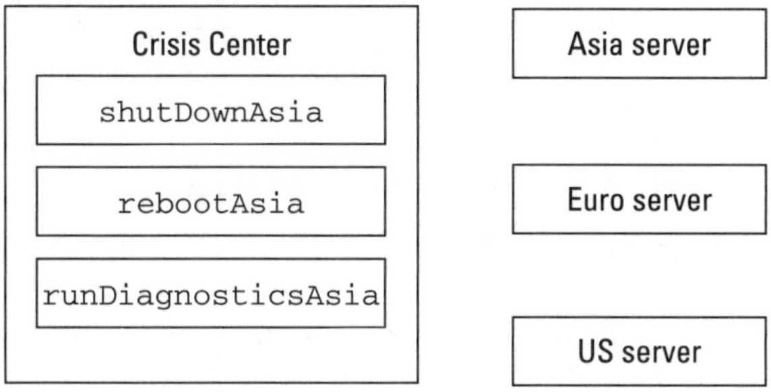

```
┌──────────────────────────┐        ┌──────────────────┐
│      Crisis Center        │        │   Asia server    │
│  ┌────────────────────┐   │        └──────────────────┘
│  │    shutDownAsia     │   │
│  └────────────────────┘   │
│  ┌────────────────────┐   │        ┌──────────────────┐
│  │     rebootAsia      │   │        │   Euro server    │
│  └────────────────────┘   │        └──────────────────┘
│  ┌────────────────────┐   │
│  │ runDiagnosticsAsia  │   │        ┌──────────────────┐
│  └────────────────────┘   │        │    US server     │
└──────────────────────────┘        └──────────────────┘
```

Figure 10-2:
The Crisis
Center's
toolkit.

In other words, the idea here is *encapsulation*. You're encapsulating a set of complex actions, targeted at a particular target, into an easily handled object. When you want to execute a command, you no longer have to take all the separate steps — connect to the target, perform the action, check on the action, and disconnect from the target. You just use the specific prebuilt, preconfigured command object, and it does the work.

The Gang of Four (GoF) book (*Design Patterns: Elements of Reusable Object-Oriented Software,* 1995, Pearson Education, Inc. Publishing as Pearson Addison Wesley) says you use the Command pattern to, "Encapsulate a request as an object, thereby letting you parameterize clients with different requests, queue or log requests, and support undoable operations."

In simple terms, the target of a command object is called its *receiver.* When you create a command object, you typically pass it the receiver it's supposed to work on so it can access that receiver. When you want to execute a command, you typically pass it to an object that acts as an *invoker.* The invoker calls the methods of the command object — such as execute (to execute the primary action on the receiver) or undo (which can undo the most recent action.

You use the Command design pattern when you've got a complex set of commands that get annoying. When the interface to those commands is so complex that it gets in the way, it makes sense to encapsulate those commands.

The inspiration behind this design pattern is that it takes encapsulation to another level. Programmers often use encapsulation to extract a set of methods and data and wrap them in an object to simplify their code. But you don't usually think of encapsulating *commands.* By preconfiguring those commands to handle the receivers of their actions and bundling complex steps into single, easy-to-handle objects, you end up with a prebuilt toolkit, ready to use. And that's what encapsulation is all about — bundling methods and data to get it out of the way. When you use this pattern, though, the objects you're creating aren't so much nouns as *verbs,* encapsulating commands.

Aiming at the target: Creating your receiver objects

The receiver is what a command object works on. In the previous example, that's one of the three company servers: the server that handles Asia, the Euro server, or the U.S. server. Each of these act as receivers of the command object's actions.

Each of these three servers has various methods, such as connect to connect to them, diagnostics to run their diagnostics, reboot, shutdown, and disconnect. Because there are three servers, you should put those methods into an interface, named, in this case, Receiver, as shown in the following:

```
public interface Receiver
{
  public void connect();
  public void diagnostics();
```

```
public void reboot();
public void shutdown();
public void disconnect();
}
```

Each receiver — that is, each server — can implement the `Receiver` inter-face. For example, here's how the `AsiaServer` class starts:

```
public class AsiaServer implements Receiver
{
        .
        .
        .
}
```

To make life a little easier, each of the server's methods can print out a mes-sage on the Crisis Center console, as shown in the following:

```
public class AsiaServer implements Receiver
{
  public AsiaServer()
  {
  }

  public void connect()
  {
    System.out.println("You're connected to the Asia server.");
  }

  public void diagnostics()
  {
    System.out.println("The Asia server diagnostics check out OK.");
  }

  public void shutdown()
  {
    System.out.println("Shutting down the Asia server.");
  }

  public void reboot()
  {
    System.out.println("Rebooting the Asia server.");
  }

  public void disconnect()
  {
    System.out.println("You're disconnected from the Asia server.");
  }

}
```

The `EuroServer` class should look like the following:

```
public class EuroServer implements Receiver
{
  public EuroServer()
  {
  }

  public void connect()
  {
    System.out.println("You're connected to the Euro server.");
  }

  public void diagnostics()
  {
    System.out.println("The Euro server diagnostics check out OK.");
  }

  public void shutdown()
  {
    System.out.println("Shutting down the Euro server.");
  }

  public void reboot()
  {
    System.out.println("Rebooting the Euro server.");
  }

  public void disconnect()
  {
    System.out.println("You're disconnected from the Euro server.");
  }

}
```

And here's the `USServer` class:

```
public class USServer implements Receiver
{
  public USServer()
  {
  }

  public void connect()
  {
    System.out.println("You're connected to the US server.");
  }

  public void diagnostics()
  {
```

```
      System.out.println("The US server diagnostics check out OK.");
  }

  public void shutdown()
  {
    System.out.println("Shutting down the US server.");
  }

  public void reboot()
  {
    System.out.println("Rebooting the US server.");
  }

  public void disconnect()
  {
    System.out.println("You're disconnected from the US server.");
  }

}
```

That gives you the three receivers that receive commands — that is, the three GlobalHugeCo servers. The next step is to create the commands that let you work with those servers.

Be the boss: Creating your commands

Commands are preconfigured to perform various actions. To make them do their thing, you typically call an execute method. Say you want three command classes here: `ShutDownCommand`, `RebootCommand`, and `RunDiagnosticsCommand`. Each of these can perform the action corresponding to its name, and each of these can be configured to work with a specific receiver. To keep things constant over these three command classes, you might set up an interface, `Command`, which supports an `execute` method.

```
public interface Command
{
  public void execute();
}
```

As with all commands, the `ShutDownCommand` class is configurable to handle a specific receiver (that is, a server in this example). This class is supposed to shut down a server, so when you create an object of this class, you pass a server to it as the command's receiver as shown in the following code:

```
public class ShutDownCommand implements Command
{
  Receiver receiver;

  public ShutDownCommand(Receiver r)
```

```
    {
        receiver = r;
    }
        .
        .
        .
}
```

When the command's `execute` method is called, it's supposed to shut down the server — which means connecting to the server, shutting it down, and then disconnecting. All that happens in the `execute` method.

```
public class ShutDownCommand implements Command
{
    Receiver receiver;

    public ShutDownCommand(Receiver r)
    {
        receiver = r;
    }

    public void execute()
    {
        receiver.connect();
        receiver.shutdown();
        receiver.disconnect();
        System.out.println();
    }
}
```

Good, you've created a configurable command class that can shut down servers. Here's the `RunDiagnosticsCommand` command class, which connects to servers, runs diagnostics on them, and then disconnects:

```
public class RunDiagnosticsCommand implements Command
{
    Receiver receiver;

    public RunDiagnosticsCommand(Receiver r)
    {
        receiver = r;
    }

    public void execute()
    {
        receiver.connect();
        receiver.diagnostics();
        receiver.disconnect();
        System.out.println();
    }
}
```

And here's the `RebootCommand` class, which reboots a server:

```
public class RebootCommand implements Command
{
  Receiver receiver;

  public RebootCommand(Receiver r)
  {
    receiver = r;
  }

  public void execute()
  {
    receiver.connect();
    receiver.reboot();
    receiver.disconnect();
    System.out.println();
  }
}
```

That gives you the receivers (that is, the three servers) and the command classes that act on those receivers. How about putting these command classes to work?

Getting your commands to actually do something: Creating the invoker

The invoker is the class that actually puts the commands to work. You typically load a command object into the invoker and tell the invoker to run it.

 When you implement the Command design pattern, you don't need to use an invoker if you don't want to — if your commands only have an `execute` method, for example, you might want to dispense with the invoker altogether and just call that method. However, as I discuss in this chapter, invokers can also keep track of multiple commands in a log or a queue, which makes undoing a sequence of commands possible.

The invoker in this example starts with only a constructor, a `setCommand` method that lets you load a command into the invoker, and a `run` method that runs the command, as you can see in the following code:

```
public class Invoker
{
  Command command;

  public Invoker()
```

```
    {
    }

    public void setCommand(Command c)
    {
       command = c;
    }

    public void run()
    {
       command.execute();
    }
}
```

You're set. You have receivers, you have the commands, you have the invoker — it's time to put this to work.

Putting commands to the test

Here's a test harness, `TestCommands.java`, which instantiates server objects and a set of commands that are ready to be used with those servers, such as `shutDownAsia`, `runDiagnosticsAsia`, and `rebootAsia`. After creating a server object, you pass it to a given command, and the command stores the server as the receiver of its actions. Then when you call the `execute` method of the command, such as `shutDownAsia`, the command calls all the necessary methods (`connect`, `shutdown`, and `disconnect`) to shut down the server it's been configured for.

You say to yourself with satisfaction: Now, when it's time to take action, the Crisis Center staff only has to load a prebuilt command into the invoker and call the invoker's `run` method to run the command. The staff no longer has to fumble around with multi-step sequences of actions that are prone to error. For example, here's how the test harness shuts down the Asia server, reboots it, runs diagnostics on it, as well as shuts down the Euro server and runs diagnostics on that server:

```
public class TestCommands
{
  public static void main(String args[])
  {
    TestCommands t = new TestCommands();
  }

  public TestCommands()
  {
    Invoker invoker = new Invoker();

    // Create the receivers
```

```
    AsiaServer asiaServer = new AsiaServer();
    EuroServer euroServer = new EuroServer();
    USServer usServer = new USServer();

    //Create the commands
    ShutDownCommand shutDownAsia = new ShutDownCommand(asiaServer);
    RunDiagnosticsCommand runDiagnosticsAsia = new
      RunDiagnosticsCommand(asiaServer);
    RebootCommand rebootAsia = new RebootCommand(asiaServer);
    ShutDownCommand shutDownEuro = new ShutDownCommand(euroServer);
    RunDiagnosticsCommand runDiagnosticsEuro = new
      RunDiagnosticsCommand(euroServer);
    RebootCommand rebootEuro = new RebootCommand(euroServer);
    ShutDownCommand shutDownUS = new ShutDownCommand(usServer);
    RunDiagnosticsCommand runDiagnosticsUS = new
      RunDiagnosticsCommand(usServer);
    RebootCommand rebootUS = new RebootCommand(usServer);

    invoker.setCommand(shutDownAsia);
    invoker.run();

    invoker.setCommand(rebootAsia);
    invoker.run();

    invoker.setCommand(runDiagnosticsAsia);
    invoker.run();

    invoker.setCommand(shutDownEuro);
    invoker.run();

    invoker.setCommand(runDiagnosticsEuro);
    invoker.run();
  }
}
```

And here's what you see when you run this code:

```
You're connected to the Asia server.
Shutting down the Asia server.
You're disconnected from the Asia server.

You're connected to the Asia server.
Rebooting the Asia server.
You're disconnected from the Asia server.

You're connected to the Asia server.
The Asia server diagnostics check out OK.
You're disconnected from the Asia server.

You're connected to the Euro server.
Shutting down the Euro server.
You're disconnected from the Euro server.
```

```
You're connected to the Euro server.
Rebooting the Euro server.
You're disconnected from the Euro server.

You're connected to the Euro server.
The Euro server diagnostics check out OK.
You're disconnected from the Euro server.
```

Excellent. Just what you wanted. Now you've got a prebuilt toolkit of commands, ready to use on the various servers.

Supporting undo

You might add an undo method to each command object to let client code undo an operation.

```
public interface Command
{
  public void execute();
  public void undo();
}
```

For example, an undo method might reboot a server in a shutdown command.

```
public class ShutDownCommand implements Command
{
  Receiver receiver;

  public ShutDownCommand(Receiver r)
  {
    receiver = r;
  }

  public void execute()
  {
    receiver.connect();
    receiver.shutdown();
    receiver.disconnect();
    System.out.println();
  }

  public void undo()
  {
    System.out.println("Undoing...");
    receiver.connect();
    receiver.reboot();
    receiver.disconnect();
    System.out.println();
  }
}
```

Why invoke the invoker?

But did you really need the invoker? All you did was call the invoker's `run` method, which called the command's `execute` method; you could have called the command's `execute` method yourself.

But take a look at the GoF definition for this pattern again: "Encapsulate a request as an object, thereby letting you parameterize clients with different requests, queue or log requests, and support undoable operations." What about that "parameterize clients with different requests"? What's that all about?

Say you had a dedicated set of invokers, each with different names — for example, one might be called `panicbutton`. When there's a problem, you don't have to think about what you're doing — you just hit the `panicbutton` invoker's `run` method. As the code enters different states, the command loaded into the `panic button` invoker may differ, but you don't have to think about that — if there's a problem, you just hit the `panicbutton` invoker's `run` method. That's one reason to use invokers.

Another reason comes from the rest of the GoF definition: " . . . queue or log requests, and support undoable operations." Invokers can keep track of entire queues of commands, which is useful if you want to start undoing sequences of commands. That's coming up next.

And when you undo a `reboot` command, you would shut down the server.

```
public class RebootCommand implements Command
{
  Receiver receiver;

  public RebootCommand(Receiver r)
  {
    receiver = r;
  }

  public void execute()
  {
    receiver.connect();
    receiver.reboot();
    receiver.disconnect();
    System.out.println();
  }

  public void undo()
  {
    System.out.println("Undoing...");
    receiver.connect();
    receiver.shutdown();
    receiver.disconnect();
    System.out.println();
  }
}
```

On the other hand, you can't really undo a run diagnostics command — once you've run the diagnostics, you can't undo them.

```java
public class RunDiagnosticsCommand implements Command
{
  Receiver receiver;

  public RunDiagnosticsCommand(Receiver r)
  {
    receiver = r;
  }

  public void execute()
  {
    receiver.connect();
    receiver.diagnostics();
    receiver.disconnect();
    System.out.println();
  }

  public void undo()
  {
    System.out.println("Can't Undo.");
    System.out.println();
  }
}
```

Now an invoker comes in handy by storing a queue of commands. If you want to undo multiple commands, you only have to call the invoker's undo method multiple times. For example, say that you want to store a maximum of five commands in the invoker, which you might do in an array. Every time a new command is loaded into the invoker, it goes into a new position in the array.

```java
public class Invoker
{
  Command commands[] = new Command[5];
  int position;

  public Invoker()
  {
    position = -1;
  }

  public void setCommand(Command c)
  {
    if (position < commands.length - 1){
      position++;
      commands[position] = c;
    } else {
```

```
    for (int loopIndex = 0; loopIndex < commands.length - 2;
      loopIndex++){
      commands[loopIndex] = commands[loopIndex + 1];
    }
    commands[commands.length - 1] = c;
  }
}
  .
  .
  .
```

Next, the invoker's `run` method should run the current command. And the invoker's `undo` method should undo the current command, and then step back one position in the command queue.

```
  .
  .
  .
public void run()
{
  commands[position].execute();
}

public void undo()
{
  if (position >= 0){
    commands[position].undo();
  }
  position--;
}
```

Testing the undo

Now you've got an invoker that can keep track of a queue of commands, which means it can perform multi-step undo operations. To test that out, you might change the test harness to shut down the Asia server, then reboot it — and then undo those two operations in sequence like this:

```
public class TestCommands
{
  public static void main(String args[])
  {
    TestCommands t = new TestCommands();
  }

public class TestCommands
{
  public static void main(String args[])
```

```
  {
    TestCommands t = new TestCommands();
  }

  public TestCommands()
  {
    Invoker invoker = new Invoker();

    // Create the receivers
    AsiaServer asiaServer = new AsiaServer();
    EuroServer euroServer = new EuroServer();
    USServer usServer = new USServer();

    //Create the commands
    ShutDownCommand shutDownAsia = new ShutDownCommand(asiaServer);
    RunDiagnosticsCommand runDiagnosticsAsia = new
      RunDiagnosticsCommand(asiaServer);
    RebootCommand rebootAsia = new RebootCommand(asiaServer);
    ShutDownCommand shutDownEuro = new ShutDownCommand(euroServer);
    RunDiagnosticsCommand runDiagnosticsEuro = new
      RunDiagnosticsCommand(euroServer);
    RebootCommand rebootEuro = new RebootCommand(euroServer);
    ShutDownCommand shutDownUS = new ShutDownCommand(usServer);
    RunDiagnosticsCommand runDiagnosticsUS = new
      RunDiagnosticsCommand(usServer);
    RebootCommand rebootUS = new RebootCommand(usServer);

    invoker.setCommand(shutDownAsia);
    invoker.run();

    invoker.setCommand(rebootAsia);
    invoker.run();

    invoker.undo();
    invoker.undo();
  }
}
```

When you run this test harness, you can see that each command is first executed and then undone in sequence.

```
You're connected to the Asia server.
Shutting down the Asia server.
You're disconnected from the Asia server.

You're connected to the Asia server.
Rebooting the Asia server.
You're disconnected from the Asia server.

Undoing...
```

```
You're connected to the Asia server.
Shutting down the Asia server.
You're disconnected from the Asia server.

Undoing...
You're connected to the Asia server.
Rebooting the Asia server.
You're disconnected from the Asia server.
```

Cool. That's what the Command design pattern is all about — encapsulating commands. As mentioned earlier, this encapsulation is a little different from the usual, where you end up with an object that you can think of as a noun. Here, you think of the resulting object more as a verb. And when you use an invoker, you can handle whole sequences of commands and undo them if needed.

Coordinating with the Mediator Pattern

"Hmm," say the programmers at agribusiness Rutabagas-R-Us Inc. "We're having trouble with our Web site."

"What's the problem?" you ask.

"There are too many pages," they say.

"How many do you have?"

"Four," they say.

"Four? That doesn't sound like too many."

"It's not really that," the programmers say. "It's the code that takes users from one page to another — what if they're on the Shopping page looking at our delicious rutabagas and want to go back to the Welcome page? Or to the Exit page? What if they're on the Purchase page, about to buy a few crates of rutabagas, but suddenly want to jump to the Exit page without buying anything? Each page has to be crammed with code that knows how to deal with other pages."

"Ah," you say, "there's no problem. I'll just put the Mediator pattern to work."

Like the Command pattern, the Mediator pattern involves coordination between objects. Figure 10-3 shows the current situation, with the four Rutabagas-R-Us Inc. Web pages: the Welcome page, the Store page for looking at the delicious rutabagas for sale, the Purchase page where you can buy fresh rutabagas to be delivered every month, and the Exit page. Note that every page has to be able to connect to every other page.

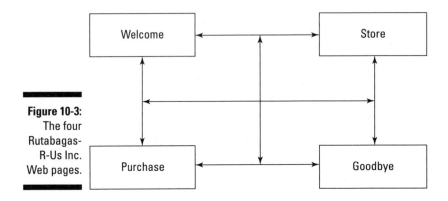

Figure 10-3:
The four
Rutabagas-
R-Us Inc.
Web pages.

The Mediator design pattern brings a central processing hub into the picture. All the pages now have to interact with the mediator only. When a page's internal state changes, it just reports that state change to the mediator, which decides where to transfer control next, acting something like a controller in Model/View/Controller architecture.

You can take the navigation code out of the separate windows and place it into the mediator object instead. The mediator can also be built to deal with each window so that the various windows don't have to know the internals of the other windows, such as which methods to call. Figure 10-4 shows how the Mediator pattern solves the traffic jam at Rutabagas-R-Us Inc.

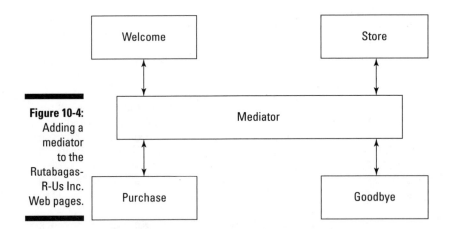

Figure 10-4:
Adding a
mediator
to the
Rutabagas-
R-Us Inc.
Web pages.

When you use a mediator, you're encapsulating the interaction between objects. Each object no longer has to know in detail how to interact with the other objects. The coupling between objects goes from tight and brittle to loose and agile. And one of the design insights of this book is that you should go for loose coupling when possible.

The Gang of Four book says you can use the Mediator pattern to, "Define an object that encapsulates how a set of objects interact. Mediator promotes loose coupling by keeping objects from referring to each other explicitly, and it lets you vary their interaction independently."

The Mediator design pattern should be your first choice as a possible solution any time you have a set of objects that are tightly coupled. If every one of a series of objects has to know the internal details of the other objects, and maintaining those relationships becomes a problem, think of the Mediator. Using a Mediator means the interaction code has to reside in only one place, and that makes it easier to maintain.

Using a mediator can hide a more serious problem: If you have multiple objects that are too tightly coupled, your encapsulation may be faulty. Might be time to rethink how you've broken your program into objects.

The Mediator pattern is something like a multiplexed Façade pattern where, instead of supplanting the interface of a single object, you're making the multiplexed interface among multiple objects easier to work with.

Designing the Rutabagas-R-Us site

Mediators are often used in GUIs, as at Rutabagas-R-Us Inc. To revamp their Web site to work with a mediator, you rewrite their Web pages to simply report state changes to the mediator. The mediator, in turn, can activate new pages by calling that page's go method.

For example, the Welcome page asks the user if he or she wants to shop or exit and, when the user makes a selection, passes the matching state change, `"welcome.shop"` or `"welcome.exit"`, to the mediator. To give the Welcome page access to the mediator, you pass the mediator object to the Welcome page's constructor. Here's what the Welcome page's code looks like:

```java
import java.io.*;

public class Welcome
{
  Mediator mediator;
  String response = "n";

  public Welcome(Mediator m)
  {
    mediator = m;
  }
```

```
public void go()
{
  System.out.print(
    "Do you want to shop? [y/n]? ");
  BufferedReader reader = new
    BufferedReader(new InputStreamReader(System.in));

  try{
    response = reader.readLine();
  } catch (IOException e){
    System.err.println("Error");
  }

  if (response.equals("y")){
    mediator.handle("welcome.shop");
  } else {
    mediator.handle("welcome.exit");
  }
}
}
```

The Shopping page displays photos of those luscious rutabagas, and from this page, the user can decide to go to the Purchase page or the Exit page.

```
import java.io.*;

public class Shop
{
  Mediator mediator;
  String response = "n";

  public Shop(Mediator m)
  {
    mediator = m;
  }

  public void go()
  {
    System.out.print(
      "Are you ready to purchase? [y/n]? ");
    BufferedReader reader = new
      BufferedReader(new InputStreamReader(System.in));

    try{
      response = reader.readLine();
    } catch (IOException e){
      System.err.println("Error");
    }

    if (response.equals("y")){
```

```
      mediator.handle("shop.purchase");
    } else {
      mediator.handle("shop.exit");
    }
  }
}
```

The Purchase page asks the user if he or she wants to buy now, and if so, thanks the user for the purchase and moves him or her to the Exit page. If the user doesn't want to buy now, the page moves him or her to the Exit page, but without displaying a message.

```java
import java.io.*;

public class Purchase
{
  Mediator mediator;
  String response = "n";

  public Purchase(Mediator m)
  {
    mediator = m;
  }

  public void go()
  {
    System.out.print(
      "Buy the item now? [y/n]? ");
    BufferedReader reader = new
      BufferedReader(new InputStreamReader(System.in));

    try{
      response = reader.readLine();
    } catch (IOException e){
      System.err.println("Error");
    }

    if (response.equals("y")){
      System.out.println("Thanks for your purchase.");
    }

    mediator.handle("purchase.exit");
  }
}
```

The Exit page just displays the following `"Please come again some-time."` message.

```
public class Exit
{
  Mediator mediator;

  public Exit(Mediator m)
  {
    mediator = m;
  }

  public void go()
  {
    System.out.println("Please come again sometime.");
  }
}
```

Those are the four pages — now it's time to connect them.

Connecting it all up with the mediator

The mediator connects all four pages together. You start the mediator by creating the individual pages and passing the mediator to its constructors so that each page has access to it.

```
public class Mediator
{
  Welcome welcome;
  Shop shop;
  Purchase purchase;
  Exit exit;

  public Mediator()
  {
    welcome = new Welcome(this);
    shop = new Shop(this);
    purchase = new Purchase(this);
    exit = new Exit(this);
  }
    .

    .

    .
```

And each page passes state changes on to the mediator's `handle` method, which calls other pages' go method as appropriate.

```
public class Mediator
{
  Welcome welcome;
  Shop shop;
  Purchase purchase;
  Exit exit;

  public Mediator()
  {
    welcome = new Welcome(this);
    shop = new Shop(this);
    purchase = new Purchase(this);
    exit = new Exit(this);
  }

  public void handle(String state)
  {
    if(state.equals("welcome.shop")){
      shop.go();
    } else if(state.equals("shop.purchase")){
      purchase.go();
    } else if(state.equals("purchase.exit")){
      exit.go();
    } else if(state.equals("welcome.exit")){
      exit.go();
    } else if(state.equals("shop.exit")){
      exit.go();
    } else if(state.equals("purchase.exit")){
      exit.go();
    }
  }

  public Welcome getWelcome()
  {
    return welcome;
  }
}
```

That's it. All that's left is to put the new mediator to the test.

Testing the Rutabagas-R-Us site

Putting this to the test is easy. Here's the test harness, `TestMediator.java`, which creates a new mediator, gets the Welcome page from the mediator, and calls the Welcome page's `go` method to get it all started.

```
public class TestMediator
{
  public static void main(String args[])
  {
    TestMediator t = new TestMediator();
  }

  public TestMediator()
  {
    Mediator mediator = new Mediator();

    mediator.getWelcome().go();
  }
}
```

The Welcome page asks the user if she wants to shop for some rutabagas.

```
Do you want to shop? [y/n]?
```

Here's a customer who's not ready to shop, and the response she gets:

```
Do you want to shop? [y/n]? n
Please come again sometime.
```

Here's a customer who's ready to shop, but doesn't want any of those succulent rutabagas:

```
Do you want to shop? [y/n]? y
Are you ready to purchase? [y/n]? n
Please come again sometime.
```

Here's a customer of the kind Rutabagas-R-Us Inc. wants to see — one who wants to purchase a few crates of rutabagas:

```
Do you want to shop? [y/n]? y
Are you ready to purchase? [y/n]? y
Buy the item now? [y/n]? y
Thanks for your purchase.
Please come again sometime.
```

As you can see, the mediator is able to coordinate all the pages. When something happens, a page lets the mediator know, and the mediator takes the appropriate next step.

Part III
The Part of Tens

The 5th Wave   By Rich Tennant

"Well, that's the third one in as many clicks. I'm sure it's just a coincidence, still, don't use the 'Launcher' again until I've had a look at it."

In this part . . .

In this part, you see ten more design patterns — the rest of the Gang of Four patterns, and some new ones that don't come from the Gang of Four. You're also going to see how to create your own design pattern from scratch. You'll see what's considered a design pattern and what's not, how to document a new one, and how to let the world know all about your new discovery.

Chapter 11

Ten More Design Patterns

"**O**kay," say the programmers at GlobalHugeCo, the computer manufacturer, "we've got the patterns you've suggested so far implemented and running. What's next?"

"Bad news," you say. "We're coming to the end of the book."

"Oh no!"

"But we're going out with a bang," you say. "This chapter contains not one, not two, but ten additional patterns."

"Woo hoo!" the programmers cry.

So far, you've seen most of the Gang of Four (GoF) patterns, but there are six more left in the original set of 23. You see those six in this chapter. They're all good patterns, but some aren't used often these days. And some are just plain hard to implement, like the Interpreter pattern, which says, "Given a language, define a representation for its grammar along with an interpreter that uses the representation to interpret sentences in the language." That sounds like a good afternoon's work.

Besides getting the remaining Gang of Four patterns, you also get a glimpse of some more modern patterns here that don't come from the GoF. These patterns are all in very common use today and come from the Portland Pattern Repository, hosted by Cunningham & Cunningham at `http://c2.com`. Anyone can get involved with these patterns, make suggestions and comments, and post all kinds of feedback. If you want to get involved with patterns and their use today, take a look at the site.

Another good patterns site is `http://hillside.net/patterns`, which maintains a Patterns Library.

Creating a Factory Factory: The Abstract Factory Pattern

In a way, the Abstract Factory pattern describes a factory of factories, or, more properly thought of, an abstract specification for an actual object factory. (If you want to know more about the plain old Factory pattern, turn to Chapter 3.) Here's the problem: Sometimes, you might need more than one factory to create objects of a similar nature. For example, say you're dealing with Swing's pluggable look-and-feel (the graphical Java package) across several different platforms. You might want to create the same application using a different look-and-feel for each, so you might want to create a number of different factories.

An Abstract Factory is usually implemented as an abstract class that real, concrete factories extend. That unifies what the concrete factories do, while allowing leeway to fit differing requirements, as when you are using a different look and feel for each application. Figure 11-1 shows how you can represent the Abstract Factory pattern.

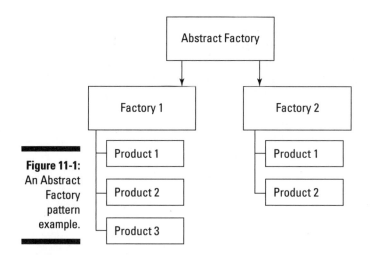

Figure 11-1:
An Abstract
Factory
pattern
example.

The GoF book (*Design Patterns: Elements of Reusable Object-Oriented Software,* 1995, Pearson Education, Inc. Publishing as Pearson Addison Wesley) says that the Abstract Factory pattern should: "Provide an interface for creating families of related or dependent objects without specifying their concrete classes."

Cloning when You Need It: The Prototype Pattern

You've been asked to help out at the local cheesecake production facility. "There's a problem," the cheesecakers say. "We're getting inundated with requests for birthday cheesecakes, where each cheesecake has to be personalized with the recipient's name on top."

"What's the problem?" you ask. "Sounds like business is good."

"The trouble is it's taking us too long to have to specify the ingredients of each cake, item by item, in our code. We can't produce enough cheesecakes — you have to call the eggs method, the creamCheese method, the bake method, the getOutOfThePan method, the. . . ."

"I get the idea," you say. "How about you just produce a single cheesecake, clone it multiple times, and then customize each one?"

"You can do that?" they ask.

"You can in Java," you say.

The Prototype pattern says that when it takes a lot of resources, or a lot of code, to create an object, you should consider simply copying an existing object and customizing it instead. In Java, you can copy objects if they have copy constructors, or you can use the clone method. Figure 11-2 illustrates how you can represent the Prototype design pattern — repeat this process as needed to create as many objects as you need.

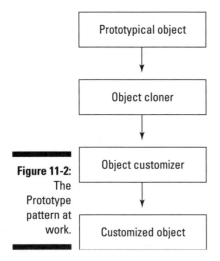

```
┌─────────────────────────┐
│   Prototypical object    │
└─────────────────────────┘
            │
            ▼
┌─────────────────────────┐
│     Object cloner        │
└─────────────────────────┘
            │
            ▼
┌─────────────────────────┐
│    Object customizer     │
└─────────────────────────┘
            │
            ▼
┌─────────────────────────┐
│    Customized object     │
└─────────────────────────┘
```

Figure 11-2:
The
Prototype
pattern at
work.

In code, all you have to do is set up a prototypical cheesecake and keep calling the `clone` method on it — no need to create a cheesecake from scratch in your code every time — and then add some customization to the new cheesecake, as needed.

The GoF book says the Prototype pattern should: "Specify the kinds of objects to create using a prototypical instance, and create new objects by copying this prototype."

Decoupling Abstractions from Implementations with the Bridge Pattern

There you are, designing car remotes for various types of cars. But it's getting confusing. You have an abstract class that's extended to create various types of car remotes: those that just control the car alarm, those that start the car remotely, and so on. But you need to deal with various different car types, such as Toyota, Honda, and so on. And to support new remotes that are planned, your abstract `Remote` class has to change as needed.

This could get pretty messy. Your abstract `Remote` class can change, and it also needs to know what type of car it's dealing with before you can extend it to create various types of remotes — in other words, the car that the remote has to work with can also change. So you've got two things that can change: your abstract `Remote` class and the `Car` implementation the remote is supposed to work with.

As you'd expect, where there are two things that can change, and they're tied together, there's a pattern that can help out. The Bridge pattern comes to the rescue by saying that you should separate out the Car type into its own class. The remote will contain a car using a "has-a" relationship so that it knows what kind of car it's dealing with. This relationship looks like the one shown in Figure 11-3 — the "has-a" connection between the remote and the car type is called the *bridge*.

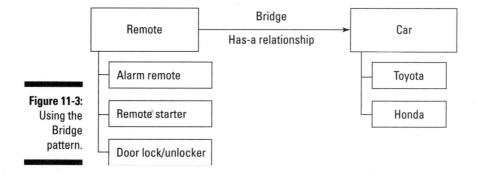

Figure 11-3: Using the Bridge pattern.

The inspiration here is that when you have an abstraction that can vary, and that's tied to an implementation that can also vary, you should decouple the two.

The GoF book says the Bridge design pattern should, "Decouple an abstraction from its implementation so that the two can vary independently."

Creating Your Own Language: The Interpreter Pattern

This is a heavy-duty pattern. It's all about putting together your own programming language, or handling an existing one, by creating an interpreter for that language.

To use this pattern, you have to know a fair bit about formal grammars to put together a language. As you can imagine, this is one of those patterns that doesn't see a lot of everyday use because creating your own language is not something many people do. For example, defining an expression in your new language might look something like the following snippet in terms of formal grammars:

```
expression ::= <command> | <repetition> | <sequence>
```

Each expression in your new language, then, might be made up of commands, repetitions of commands, and sequences expressions. Each item might be represented as an object with an `interpret` method to translate your new language into something you can run in Java, as shown in Figure 11-4.

Figure 11-4:
An example showing the Interpreter pattern.

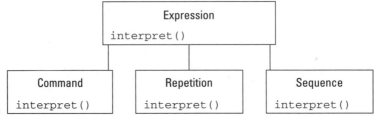

Needless to say, implementing this pattern can get very involved. I cover it here for completeness, but as you can imagine, it's not one you want to start tangling with on a daily basis.

The GoF book says the Interpreter pattern should, "Given a language, define a representation for its grammar along with an interpreter that uses the representation to interpret sentences in the language."

Forget Me Not: The Memento Pattern

"Oh no!" cries the CEO. "The database crashed and we lost a lot of data."

"What kind of data?" you ask.

"Oh," says the CEO slyly, "salary and payment information, mostly — all the data that will let us pay you for your consulting work here."

"Don't worry about it," you say, pulling out a flash drive stick and plugging it into a networked machine. "I've been studying the Memento design pattern and have a nice, private backup object that's saved the database's state. It'll be easy to undo the problem."

"Swell," says the CEO glumly.

Here's the problem. The client code has total access to the database, as outlined in Figure 11-5, so if someone flubs an operation, the database is in danger.

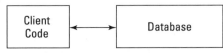

The GoF comes to the rescue with the Memento design pattern, which gives you a way to restore an object's state.

The GoF book says that the Memento pattern is designed to, "Without violating encapsulation, capture and externalize an object's internal state so that the object can be restored to this state later."

More than just a save-state undo command, the idea here is to "capture and externalize an object's internal state" for backup. You might do that with a save-state object accessible from both the client code and the database, as shown in Figure 11-6.

Figure 11-6:
Saving an
object's
state.

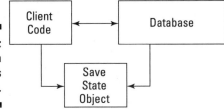

That solution, however, violates the database's encapsulation, and the Memento design pattern starts off by saying, "Without violating encapsulation. . . ."

So what do you do? You make the save-state object private to the database, as illustrated in Figure 11-7.

Figure 11-7: A private save-state object.

Now the save-state object is inaccessible outside of the database — you're not violating the database's encapsulation. That's the Memento design pattern — using it, you can create save-state objects that enable commands like undo, without violating the main object's encapsulation.

The Visitor Stops In for a Moment

If you read Chapter 8, remember the Composite you built to hold the corporate structure of GiantDataPool Inc., with all the divisions and vice presidents? Well, now the CEO is back with a problem. "They say I can only fire the vice presidents who have been here less than a year, so I need you to alter the Composite."

"Yes?" you ask.

"Each object in the Composite tree structure already has a hireDate method that returns the hire date of each vice president. I want you to add a new method named fireable that returns true if the vice president has been here less than a year. And do the same for all the directors and managers that have been added to the composite as well."

"Hmm," you say, "that means changing the VP, Director, and Manager classes to add the new fireable method. Might be easier just to use the Visitor design pattern."

"And cheaper?" asks the CEO.

"Not cheaper," you say.

With the Visitor design pattern, you can add a new operation to a structure of objects, like a Composite structure, without changing the objects in the structure. A `visitor` object moves from object to object in the structure, visiting each one and capturing its state. When the visitor has captured all the data it needs from the objects in the structure it's visiting, you can call the methods of the visitor, such as the `fireable` method that will return a list of personnel eligible for termination of employment.

The GoF book says the Visitor pattern should, "Represent an operation to be performed on the elements of an object structure. Visitor lets you define a new operation without changing the classes of the elements on which it operates."

In practice, you usually use a traverser object of some kind that can move around the object structure whose data you want, feeding data to the `Visitor` object like this, where the `Visitor` is acquiring data about GiantDataPool Inc, as shown in the Figure 11-8.

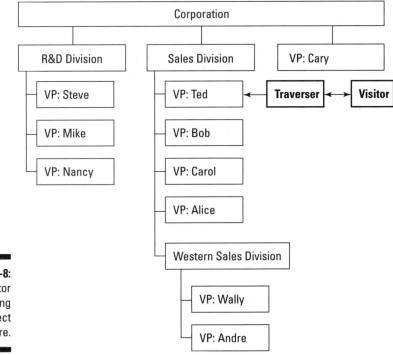

Figure 11-8:
A visitor traversing an object structure.

The traverser moves the `Visitor` object from item to item in the Composite, as shown in Figure 11-9.

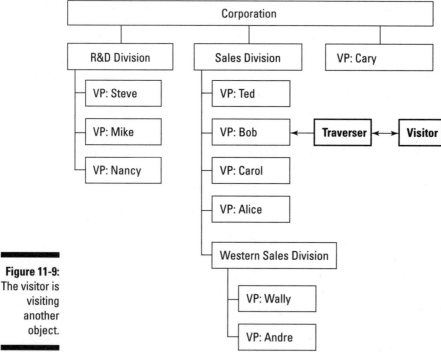

Figure 11-9:
The visitor is visiting another object.

Alternatively, you can build the traverser into the `Visitor` object. Note that while this works — the `Visitor` can move over the entire object structure, gathering information, and you can then interrogate the `Visitor` about the information it's gathered — it violates the encapsulation of the objects in the structure. Naughty, naughty.

That completes the 23 GoF design patterns — now you've seen them all.

In the rest of this chapter, I take a look at additional design patterns from the Portland Pattern Repository, as hosted by Cunningham & Cunningham at http://c2.com.

Going in Circles with Circular Buffers

"Here's another problem," say the company programmers at GiantDataPool Inc. "We've got data coming in on this line and going out on that line."

"So what's the problem?" you ask.

"How the heck do we store that data?" they ask. "We keep running out of space."

"Try a circular buffer," you say. "It's perfect when one part of your code stores data and another part reads that data asynchronously. Makes very efficient use of memory."

According to the Portland Pattern Repository's definition of the Circular Buffer design patterns, "A circular buffer is a memory allocation scheme where memory is reused (reclaimed) when an index, incremented modulo the buffer size, writes over a previously used location. A circular buffer makes a bounded queue when separate indices are used for inserting and removing data. The queue can be safely shared between threads (or processors) without further synchronization so long as one processor enqueues data and the other dequeues it." — `http://c2.com/cgi/wiki?CircularBuffer`

Take a look at Figure 11-10 to see how a circular buffer, also called a *ring buffer,* works. You store data items in the various locations in a ring buffer and keep track of reading and writing operations by labeling one location the *head* and one the *tail.*

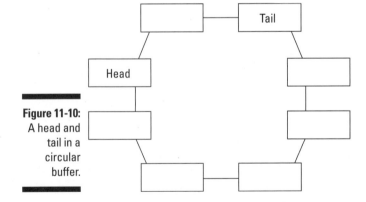

Figure 11-10:
A head and tail in a circular buffer.

When you store an item in the circular buffer, you store the item at the tail location, and the tail advances to the next location, as you can see in Figure 11-11.

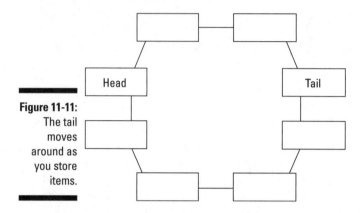

When you read an item, you read the item at the current head location, and the head advances to the next position (see Figure 11-12).

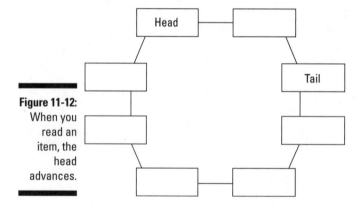

By writing to the tail and reading from the head, two streams can store and read data from the same circular buffer at the same time. The following code illustrates an example, `CircularBuffer.java`, which sets up an array holding the number of items you pass to the constructor.

```java
public class CircularBuffer
{
    private Integer data[];
    private int head;
    private int tail;

    public CircularBuffer(Integer number)
```

```
    {
      data = new Integer[number];
      head = 0;
      tail = 0;
    }
      .
      .
      .
  }
```

The `store` method stores an item and advances the tail.

```
public class CircularBuffer
{
  private Integer data[];
  private int head;
  private int tail;

  public CircularBuffer(Integer number)
  {
    data = new Integer[number];
    head = 0;
    tail = 0;
  }

  public boolean store(Integer value)
  {
    if (!bufferFull()) {
        data[tail++] = value;
        if(tail == data.length){
          tail = 0;
        }
        return true;
    } else {
        return false;
    }
  }
    .
    .
    .

  private boolean bufferFull()
  {
    if(tail + 1 == head){
      return true;
    }
    if(tail == (data.length - 1) && head == 0){
      return true;
    }
    return false;
  }
}
```

And the `read` method reads the item at the head location, and advances the head, as you can see here:

```java
public class CircularBuffer
{
  private Integer data[];
  private int head;
  private int tail;

  public CircularBuffer(Integer number)
  {
    data = new Integer[number];
    head = 0;
    tail = 0;
  }
      .
      .
      .
  public Integer read()
  {
    if (head != tail) {
      int value = data[head++];
      if(head == data.length){
        head = 0;
      }
      return value;
    } else {
      return null;
    }
  }
      .
      .
      .
}
```

Want to give this a test spin? Try `TestCircularBuffer.java` (see the Introduction for the Web address where you can get this), which loads the circular buffer with data and reads it.

```java
public class TestCircularBuffer
{
  public static void main(String args[])
  {
    TestCircularBuffer t = new TestCircularBuffer();
  }

  public TestCircularBuffer()
  {
    CircularBuffer c = new CircularBuffer(8);

    System.out.println("Storing: 1");
```

```
        c.store(1);
        System.out.println("Reading: " + c.read());
        System.out.println("Storing: 2");
        c.store(2);
        System.out.println("Storing: 3");
        c.store(3);
        System.out.println("Storing: 4");
        c.store(4);
        System.out.println("Reading: " + c.read());
        System.out.println("Storing: 5");
        c.store(5);
        System.out.println("Storing: 6");
        c.store(6);
        System.out.println("Storing: 7");
        c.store(7);
        System.out.println("Reading: " + c.read());
        System.out.println("Storing: 8");
        c.store(8);
        System.out.println("Storing: 9");
        c.store(9);
        System.out.println("Storing: 10");
        c.store(10);
        System.out.println("Storing: 11");
        c.store(11);
        System.out.println("Storing: 12");
        c.store(12);
        System.out.println("Reading: " + c.read());
        System.out.println("Reading: " + c.read());
        System.out.println("Reading: " + c.read());
        System.out.println("Reading: " + c.read());
        System.out.println("Reading: " + c.read());
        System.out.println("Reading: " + c.read());
        System.out.println("Reading: " + c.read());
        System.out.println("Reading: " + c.read());
    }
}
```

When you run `TestCircularBuffer.java`, you see the following output;
note that the buffer fills up when the test code stores a value of 10 — the
values after that point aren't stored because no data has been read from the
buffer to make room. That means that when you try to read the values past
10, you simply get `null`. (The `CircularBuffer` class handles its data internally as `Integer` objects, not `int` values, to be able to return `null` values if
the buffer is empty.)

```
Storing: 1
Reading: 1
Storing: 2
Storing: 3
Storing: 4
```

```
Reading: 2
Storing: 5
Storing: 6
Storing: 7
Reading: 3
Storing: 8
Storing: 9
Storing: 10
Storing: 11
Storing: 12
Reading: 4
Reading: 5
Reading: 6
Reading: 7
Reading: 8
Reading: 9
Reading: 10
Reading: null
```

Do circular buffers exist in Java as it stands? They sure do — take a look at the `PipedInputStream` and `PipedOutputStream` classes in the Java documentation. You connect a piped input stream to a piped output stream, and the result acts like a circular buffer. You write to the piped output stream in one thread and read from the piped input stream in another thread.

Doing Your Magic Off-Screen with the Double Buffer Pattern

The Portland Pattern Repository also includes a definition for the Double Buffer design pattern. You may have come across this one before; double buffering is often used in Java to avoid screen flicker when you're displaying graphics. The idea is that you perform your multi-step graphics creation off-screen in a buffer and then flash the results on the screen when they're complete. The process is called *double buffering* because the screen display buffer is one buffer and the buffer in which the images are prepared is the second buffer.

Figure 11-13 gives you an idea of how the process works.

Figure 11-13:
An overview of double buffering.

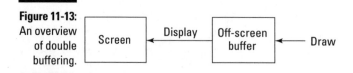

Regarding the Double Buffer design patterns, the Portland Pattern Repository makes the following recommendation: "Use a DoubleBuffer, i.e. two buffers, when generating revised datasets for an asynchronous processor. When the new data is complete and self consistent, redirect the asynchronous processor to the alternate buffer." — `http://c2.com/cgi/wiki?DoubleBuffer`

Will you find any support for double buffering in Java? Yep, you can find double buffering sprinkled all around Java. One of the primary places you find double buffering is in the `Component` class's `createImage` method, which is often used for double buffering. Here's how this method is defined in the Java 1.5 documentation:

"Image Component.createImage(int width, int height) Creates an off-screen drawable image to be used for double buffering."

The idea is that you use `createImage` to create an `Image` object compatible with a particular visual component in your application and draw in that `Image` object. When you want to flash the completed image onscreen, you can use a `Graphics` object's `drawImage` method.

How about an example showing `createImage` at work? `DoubleBuffer.java` in the downloadable code for this book (see the Introduction for the Web address where you can get that) shows how this works. It uses a worker thread to draw a set of increasingly deeper red rectangles off-screen and then flashes them onscreen.

The `main` method creates the window and gets everything started by creating and displaying a window, then calling the `drawGraphics` method to display the rectangles.

```
import java.awt.*;
import java.awt.event.*;

public class DoubleBuffer extends Frame implements Runable
{
  Image image;
  Thread thread;
  Graphics graphics = null;
  int loopIndex = 0;

  public static void main(String [] args)
  {
    DoubleBuffer d = new DoubleBuffer();

    d.setSize(200, 200);
```

```
     d.addWindowListener(new WindowAdapter() {public void
        windowClosing(WindowEvent e) {System.exit(0);}});

     d.setTitle("Double buffering example");

     d.setVisible(true);

     d.drawGraphics();
   }

   public DoubleBuffer()
   {
   }
```

The `drawGraphics` method creates the `Image` object for double buffering and gets a `Graphics` object for that image to do the actual drawing. It also starts the worker thread, which repaints the window ten times a second in the `run` method.

```
   public void drawGraphics()
   {
      image = createImage(100, 100);
      graphics = image.getGraphics();
      thread = new Thread(this);
      thread.start();
   }

   public void run()
   {
      while(true){
        repaint();
        try {Thread.sleep(100);}
        catch(InterruptedException e) {System.err.println(e);}
      }
   }
```

Every time the `repaint` method is called, the window calls the `paint` method, which is where the rectangles are drawn in the `Image` object double buffer and then copied to the screen with the `drawImage` method.

```
   public void paint (Graphics g)
   {
      if(graphics != null){
        loopIndex += 4;
        if(loopIndex >= 100){
          loopIndex = 4;
        }
        graphics.setColor(new Color(255, 255, 255));
        graphics.fillRect(0, 0, 100, 100);
```

```
        graphics.setColor(new Color(2 * loopIndex, 0, 0));
        graphics.drawRect(0, 0, loopIndex, loopIndex);

        g.drawImage(image, 60, 60, this);
    }
  }
}
```

There you go — the images are drawn off-screen in a new buffer and then transferred onscreen as needed.

Getting Multiple-Use Objects Out of the Recycle Bin Design Pattern

If your code uses many objects and the object-creation process is time- and resource-intensive, you might want to use the Recycle Bin design pattern. The idea is that when you're done with an object, you toss it into the recycle bin, and when you need an object of the same kind again, you can grab it out of the recycle bin. Figure 11-14 shows how this pattern works, in overview.

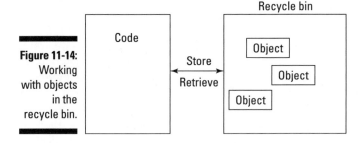

Figure 11-14:
Working
with objects
in the
recycle bin.

The Portland Pattern Repository's definition of the Recycle Bin design pattern is as follows: "You can store freed resources in a local bin so that subsequent requests for these resources can reuse the ones in the bin. A client requests resources through the bin. The bin will reuse an existing one if available or create a new one if necessary. The recycle bin may request more resources than actually needed to optimize performance. When the use of the resource is complete, it should be returned to the bin." — http://c2.com/cgi/wiki?RecycleBin

You can also find recycle bins in Java, such as in the thread pooling that you can configure using classes like `ScheduledThreadPoolExecutor` and `ThreadPoolExecutor`.

Entering the Big Time with the Model/View/Controller Pattern

Another popular design pattern you see at the Portland Pattern Repository is the Model/View/Controller, or MVC, design pattern. This pattern represents a good design insight: separating the code used for presentation from that which works on and handles data. Very often, Java-based online applications are written with a few JavaServer Pages (JSPs), and JSP is notorious for mixing presentation code (including HTML) with logic code (Java code).

Larger online Java applications, particularly those based on an application framework like Jakarta Struts, very often use MVC architecture these days. The *controller* (which is often a Java servlet) oversees the whole application, calling code in the *model* (often a JavaBean) to handle the internal logic and business rules and then sending the results to the presentation layer, the *view* (often made up of JSPs), which interacts with the user. Here's an overview of these three components:

- **Model:** Implements the data crunching of the application. This is the core code that does the application's internal work. The model doesn't know anything about the view or the controller — you just pass it data and it goes from there, returning its results. In online Java applications, the model is often implemented using JavaBeans.

- **View:** Implements the presentation layer that interacts with the user. When the user starts interacting with an online Java application, the Web page(s) they see are part of the view. The view also takes data supplied to it (usually from the controller) and displays it. In online Java applications, the view is often implemented using JSP.

- **Controller:** Acts as the boss of the application and is responsible for routing data to the right model and view components. The controller oversees the model and the view by reacting to the data the user sends. In online Java applications, the controller is often implemented as a servlet.

Figure 11-15 provides a schematic overview of MVC architecture:

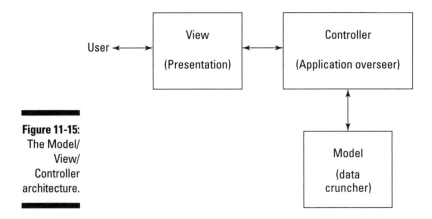

Figure 11-15:
The Model/
View/
Controller
architecture.

The Portland Pattern Repository says that the Model/View/Controller design pattern is, "A triad of three modules linked by the ObserverPattern, all residing within a RepresentationLayer. The View drives a presentation within a GUILayer, and elements within the View observe the Model. Elements within the Controller observe the View and Model, and elements within the Model observe the Controller. The Model fronts data objects within the LogicLayer. This pattern decouples changes to how data are manipulated from how they are displayed or stored, while unifying the code in each component." — http://c2.com/cgi/wiki?ModelViewController

If you're interested in creating MVC applications in Java, take a look at the Jakarta Struts application framework at http://struts.apache.org. This framework does a lot of the work for you, including setting up a standard controller servlet that you can customize by creating your own objects based on the Struts Action class, which you can pass to the controller. For more on this topic, see *Jakarta Struts for Dummies,* by Mike Robinson and Ellen Finkelstein (Wiley Publishing, Inc.).

Chapter 12

Ten Easy Steps to Create Your Own Patterns

· ·

In This Chapter

▶ Introducing the pattern catalog style

▶ Understanding the Rule of Three standard

▶ Creating your own pattern

▶ Sharing your pattern with others

· ·

Suddenly, there's a terrific roar on the grounds of Missiles-N-Stuff, the company where you've been hired as a consultant. As you watch, a missile thunders off over the horizon.

"Darn," say the Missiles-N-Stuff programmers. "That one wasn't supposed to go off."

"Isn't it heading towards town?" you ask.

"Yep," they say, "but don't worry about it. They're used to evacuations. The real problem is our code. Somehow we just can't make sure that missiles don't go off by accident. The code's gotten too large to handle it easily — everything's become too interwoven. Isn't there a design pattern that will help us out?"

"Nope," you say, "but you can invent one."

This Part of Tens chapter gives you a guide for how to build your own pattern in ten easy steps. Just follow along, and you're on the route to fame and fortune (well, maybe not fame . . . and the fortune part isn't all that sure either. . . .).

The Rule of Three

Design patterns were actually invented by Christopher Alexander, an architect at Berkeley. His book on the topic is named *A Pattern Language: Towns, Buildings, Construction* (Oxford University Press), and it deals with architectural, not computing, problems. So you can have design patterns in any field.

And if you can abstract such a pattern, why not share it? For example, say you're a painter who specializes in painting porch floors. That's all you paint, and you're the best at it. But sometimes you paint yourself into a corner. You notice that this happens when you've left yourself only one way out and then paint over it. So you come up with a new design pattern for porch painters: "Always leave yourself a way out when approaching corners. And don't paint over it." Not bad, you think, and post it all over the Internet for the benefit of other porch painters.

Are you a little premature in doing that? Could be. Patterns generally are expected to pass the "Rule of Three" before they can be taken seriously. The Rule of Three says that a pattern has to be used in at least three real-world applications before it can be considered for true patternhood. In fact, it's even a little more rigorous than that — these days, you list ten criteria for a new pattern and enter it into a *pattern catalog*. (See the "Following the Pattern Catalog Style" section in this chapter for more information on pattern catalogs.)

Don't see an established design pattern where you think there should be one? You can create your own design pattern, and you can publicize that pattern, getting it into design pattern repositories around the world, leading to international fame (if not necessarily fortune).

Don't forget — design patterns are supposed to make solutions easier. Don't create a design pattern just for the sake of creating a new pattern if it's not going to be helpful. After all, patterns are supposed to be tools, not hindrances.

A design pattern, after all, is just a solution to a particular class of problem. The idea is to create a pattern that uses good object-oriented programming practices and that offers a solution template for a commonly encountered problem.

Technically speaking, the goals and constraints that a pattern works with are called forces by design pattern designers. I won't use that term in the discussion here, but if you start designing patterns for a living, don't be surprised if you come across it.

Following the Pattern Catalog Style

The best way to start anything is with a guide of some kind, and for design patterns, that guide is the pattern catalog style. There are ten sections in a pattern catalog, and here they are — you're going to see a definition of each of these in the remainder of this chapter.

1. Intent

2. Motivation

3. Applicability

4. Structure

5. Participants

6. Collaborations

7. Consequences

8. Implementation/Sample Code

9. Known Uses

10. Related Patterns

In the Gang of Four (GoF) book (*Design Patterns: Elements of Reusable Object-Oriented Software,* 1995, Pearson Education, Inc. Publishing as Pearson Addison Wesley), each of the 23 patterns is written in catalog style, with each of these ten topics carefully covered for each pattern in the GoF book.

When you want to create a pattern for formal submission to the pattern-using community, you start by giving your new pattern a name, and then you can write about the pattern's intent, motivation, applicability, and so on.

Introducing the Veto Pattern

How's creating a pattern work in practice? I take a look at the Missiles-N-Stuff problem mentioned at the beginning of the chapter as an example, creating a new pattern here on the fly.

The programmers' problem is that their code had gotten too unmanageable, and you (the brilliant design pattern expert) start thinking about it. You come to the conclusion that they should encapsulate the components that need to approve firing a missile. Encapsulating the components of the code that have to approve a missile launch into their own objects means that they won't interfere with each other. The idea is that instead of a mass of interrelated code where who's doing what isn't clear, you now have a number of discrete, self-contained objects that all have to agree before the missile is launched.

Encapsulating each yes/no condition into its own object cleans up the code. And by connecting the objects into a chain, you can make sure that each object has its chance to say no if it wants to — to get a request approved, that request has to pass through the entire chain.

So you now have a discrete set of objects, all of which have to approve a missile launch before it happens. And if any one of those objects says no, the launch doesn't happen. In other words, any one of these objects can veto the launch, so let's call this new pattern the Veto pattern — does that sound catchy enough?

Alright, now that the pattern has a name, it's time to fill in the ten topics that you need to enter this pattern into a pattern catalog, starting with the pattern's *intent*.

1. Intent

The Intent design pattern catalog entry describes the pattern and what it's supposed to do. This is a short overview of the pattern that someone is supposed to be able to read and understand to know if the pattern solves her problem.

So how *does* your new Veto pattern work? Each object has to approve an action, such as a missile launch, before it can occur, so you can arrange the objects into a chain. Each object becomes a mission-critical link in the chain, and each link has to approve a request before the request is approved overall. Here's how you might write the Intent of the Veto pattern:

"Process a veto-able request by sending it through a chain of encapsulated objects, each of which can veto that request."

 When you write the intent of a pattern, keep it simple, even if it means not including every little detail. This is an overview of your pattern, sort of like the descriptions in *TV Guide,* that lets readers know if they're going to be interested in your pattern.

2. Motivation

The Motivation section of a design pattern catalog entry lists a scenario that describes the problem the pattern is supposed to solve, using a concrete scenario.

In this example, you might phrase that this way:

"Say you're in charge of a missile-launch system, and that three separate mission-critical components must confirm a missile launch before it happens. If those components are part of a monolithic program, they can be interwoven in unexpected ways, and the result is that unclear code may launch missiles when they shouldn't be launched. For maximum clarity of action, separate the components that will decide the missile launch and chain them as encapsulated links, each one of which must agree to the launch in succession before it can occur."

3. Applicability

The Applicability section of a pattern's catalog entry describes general scenarios where a pattern can be applied. You usually provide a set of conditions — and if a problem meets those conditions, your pattern is a good candidate to solve it.

For example, for your new Veto pattern, you might say the following:

"If you have a situation where you have mission-critical components that may conflict with one another when in the same piece of code, this pattern may be a good one for you. If you don't want to undertake an action unless several well-defined criteria are met, the Veto pattern may help."

4. Structure

The Structure section of a pattern in a pattern catalog usually shows a diagram indicating how the pattern works. In the case of the Veto pattern, you want to arrange the objects that can veto a request as links in a chain, each of which has to approve before a particular action can be taken. You might draw the diagram for this pattern as shown in Figure 12-1.

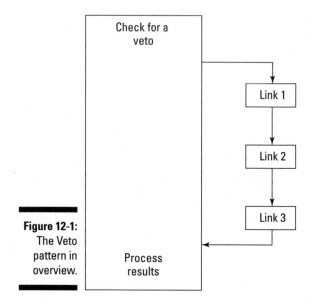

Figure 12-1:
The Veto
pattern in
overview.

As you can see, the idea here is that you send a request through all the links in the object chain and if any one of the links vetoes the request, the request is denied.

5. Participants

The Participants section of a pattern's catalog entry lists the classes and objects that take part in the pattern, as well as their roles. To create the link objects in the veto chain, for instance, you might want to make sure they all use the same methods — so you should have a Link interface. And you should list the Link classes here that implement that interface, as well as the client code that attempts to send requests through the chain of links.

Here's how you might list the participants in the Veto pattern:

- **Link interface:** Lists the methods you want each link in the veto chain to implement.

- **Link objects:** Each link in the chain represents an object that can veto the request being sent through the chain.

- **Client code:** The client code sends a request to the first link in the chain, which sends it on to the next link and so on, until the result is sent back to the client code.

6. Collaborations

The Collaborations section of a pattern's catalog entry indicates how the participants (listed in the previous section) work together.

In the case of the Veto pattern, that might look something like this:

"You use the Link interface to specify the methods that each link in the veto chain must implement. After creating a chain of links, you send a request from the client code to the first link, which passes the request on to the next link, which passes it on to the next link after that, and so on. The request is passed in this way from link to link — if any link vetoes the request, all following links must pass that veto on to the client code. The last link passes the results back to the client code. Because the request is passed in sequence from link to link, all links in the chain get the chance to veto the request if needed."

7. Consequences

The Consequences section of a pattern's catalog entry lists both the good and bad effects of the pattern. Your pattern, being the most advanced and excellent one the world has yet seen, may not have any apparent drawbacks, but think hard on this point — it wouldn't be good if you steered someone into using your pattern if that pattern's going to cause him or her problems.

For your new Veto pattern, you might say:

"The consequence of this pattern is that it allows you to encapsulate the voting objects so that any object may make its decisions independently of the code in other objects, and any object may veto a request. You are also assured that each link in the object chain gets a chance to veto a request before sending it on to the next object.

On the other hand, encapsulating all the decision-making components into discrete objects can be a problem because doing so can deny one object needed information from the rest of the objects. If that's the case in your implementation, consider combining two or more link objects into one as needed so that encapsulation won't be violated.

Another potential problem comes when one object in the chain of objects doesn't pass on a veto correctly. Because the objects are in a chain, you're dependent on the correct functioning of each link in the chain to get the proper results."

8. Implementation/Sample Code

The Implementation/Sample Code section of a pattern's entry in a pattern catalog outlines the techniques you use when implementing this pattern and/or sample code.

For the Veto design pattern, you might say something like this:

"When you want to check if a request will be accepted or vetoed, give each link (and the Link interface) a method that will be passed a Boolean value. If any link vetoes the request, that link should pass a value of false to the next link in the chain, and any such veto should be passed on by having each subsequent link in the chain pass on a value of false if it was passed a value of false. The last link in the chain should be connected back to the client code so that that code may receive the results of the accept/veto process.

Here's some sample code that implements the new Veto pattern. Each link in the chain can veto a request sent to it, and in this example, it's simply passed a Boolean true/false value to a method named check that must be implemented by each link. Here's what that method looks like in the Link interface:

```
public interface Link
{
    public void check(boolean b);
}
```

To connect the links in a chain, you pass the next link in the chain to the current link's constructor when you instantiate the current link. The following code shows what that looks like in the Link1 class, the first of the links in our chain, which implements the Link interface:

```
public class Link1 implements Link
{
    Link next;

    public Link1(Link n)
    {
        next = n;
    }

        .
        .
        .

}
```

If the link's check method is passed a value of true, this link just passes that value along to the next link in the chain.

```
public class Link1 implements Link
{
  Link next;

  public Link1(Link n)
  {
    next = n;
  }

  public void check(boolean b)
  {
    if(b){
      next.check(true);
        .
        .
        .

  }
}
```

On the other hand, if the check method is passed a value of false, meaning some link in the chain has already vetoed the request, this link should pass on that veto by calling the next link's check method with a value of false.

```
public class Link1 implements Link
{
  Link next;

  public Link1(Link n)
  {
    next = n;
  }

  public void check(boolean b)
  {
    if(b){
      next.check(true);
    } else {
      next.check(false);
    }
  }
}
```

The Link2 class also does the same.

```
public class Link2 implements Link
{
  Link next;

  public Link2(Link n)
  {
```

```
    next = n;
  }

  public void check(boolean b)
  {
    if(b){
      next.check(true);
    } else {
      next.check(false);
    }
  }
}
```

. . . as does the `Link3` class.

```
public class Link3 implements Link
{
  Link next;

  public Link3(Link n)
  {
    next = n;
  }

  public void check(boolean b)
  {
    if(b){
      next.check(true);
    } else {
      next.check(false);
    }
  }
}
```

Use the client code, `TestVeto.java`, to test this out. This client code is passed the results of the veto chain, which means that it should implement the `Link` interface itself, allowing it to be passed to the last link in the chain.

```
public class TestVeto implements Link
{
    .
    .
    .
}
```

Here's how you form a chain of three links and connect them:

```
public class TestVeto implements Link
{
  Link link1, link2, link3;

  public static void main(String args[])
```

```
  {
    TestVeto t = new TestVeto();
  }

public TestVeto()
{
  link3 = new Link3(this);
  link2 = new Link2(link3);
  link1 = new Link1(link2);
}
    .
    .
    .
}
```

You've created the link of objects that can veto the request — all you need to do now is send that request through the link of objects, and this code does that with a method called getOK, which is called from the constructor, and which sends a value of true to the first link.

```
public class TestVeto implements Link
{
  Link link1, link2, link3;

  public static void main(String args[])
  {
    TestVeto t = new TestVeto();
  }

  public TestVeto()
  {
    link3 = new Link3(this);
    link2 = new Link2(link3);
    link1 = new Link1(link2);

    getOK();
  }

  public void getOK()
  {
    link1.check(true);
  }
    .
    .
    .
}
```

The client is passed the results by the last link in the chain, which calls the check method of the client code. If the value passed to the check method is true, the request is accepted — if the value is `false`, however, the request is vetoed. Here's how the client code indicates the results:

```
public class TestVeto implements Link
{
  Link link1, link2, link3;

  public static void main(String args[])
  {
    TestVeto t = new TestVeto();
  }

  public TestVeto()
  {
    link3 = new Link3(this);
    link2 = new Link2(link3);
    link1 = new Link1(link2);

    getOK();
  }

  public void getOK()
  {
    link1.check(true);
  }

  public void check(boolean b)
  {
    if(b){
      System.out.println("OK");
    } else {
      System.out.println("Not OK");
    }
  }
}
```

When you run this test, the results show that the request is granted:

```
OK
```

Very nice.

9. Known Uses

The Known Uses section of a pattern's catalog entry gives some real-world examples where the pattern has been used. In this case, you may have already put your Veto pattern to work in several applications and/or seen it in other applications. Or you may just have watched presidential vetoes on the news. In any case, bear in mind the Rule of Three (see the sidebar earlier in the chapter) — you should have three real-world applications to list here in the Known Uses section.

10. Related Patterns

Finally, the Related Patterns section lists other patterns that might be related to this one. For example, you might consider the Veto pattern to be a cousin of the GoF Chain of Responsibility pattern, where a request is sent down a chain of objects until one of the objects handles the request. That's similar to your Veto pattern — it's related but distinct (for one thing, requests have to pass all the way through the object chain in the Veto pattern). So you might list that pattern in this section.

And that's it. Congratulations — you've created your own new pattern. All you've got to do now is to submit your new pattern catalog entry to a design patterns repository.

Getting Your Pattern into a Pattern Catalog

How do you tell people about your pattern? You list your pattern in a pattern catalog, which is then stored in a pattern repository, such as the Portland Pattern Repository, as hosted by Cunningham & Cunningham at `http://c2.com`. (I cover some of the patterns supported by the Portland Patterns Repository in Chapter 11.)

Index

• *U* •

• *V* •

• W •

• X •

Notes

Notes

Notes

Notes

Notes

Notes

BUSINESS, CAREERS & PERSONAL FINANCE

0-7645-5307-0

0-7645-5331-3 *†

Also available:

- Accounting For Dummies †
  0-7645-5314-3
- Business Plans Kit For Dummies †
  0-7645-5365-8
- Cover Letters For Dummies
  0-7645-5224-4
- Frugal Living For Dummies
  0-7645-5403-4
- Leadership For Dummies
  0-7645-5176-0
- Managing For Dummies
  0-7645-1771-6

- Marketing For Dummies
  0-7645-5600-2
- Personal Finance For Dummies *
  0-7645-2590-5
- Project Management For Dummies
  0-7645-5283-X
- Resumes For Dummies †
  0-7645-5471-9
- Selling For Dummies
  0-7645-5363-1
- Small Business Kit For Dummies *†
  0-7645-5093-4

HOME & BUSINESS COMPUTER BASICS

0-7645-4074-2

0-7645-3758-X

Also available:

- ACT! 6 For Dummies
  0-7645-2645-6
- iLife '04 All-in-One Desk Reference
  For Dummies
  0-7645-7347-0
- iPAQ For Dummies
  0-7645-6769-1
- Mac OS X Panther Timesaving
  Techniques For Dummies
  0-7645-5812-9
- Macs For Dummies
  0-7645-5656-8

- Microsoft Money 2004 For Dummies
  0-7645-4195-1
- Office 2003 All-in-One Desk Reference
  For Dummies
  0-7645-3883-7
- Outlook 2003 For Dummies
  0-7645-3759-8
- PCs For Dummies
  0-7645-4074-2
- TiVo For Dummies
  0-7645-6923-6
- Upgrading and Fixing PCs For Dummies
  0-7645-1665-5
- Windows XP Timesaving Techniques
  For Dummies
  0-7645-3748-2

FOOD, HOME, GARDEN, HOBBIES, MUSIC & PETS

0-7645-5295-3

0-7645-5232-5

Also available:

- Bass Guitar For Dummies
  0-7645-2487-9
- Diabetes Cookbook For Dummies
  0-7645-5230-9
- Gardening For Dummies *
  0-7645-5130-2
- Guitar For Dummies
  0-7645-5106-X
- Holiday Decorating For Dummies
  0-7645-2570-0
- Home Improvement All-in-One
  For Dummies
  0-7645-5680-0

- Knitting For Dummies
  0-7645-5395-X
- Piano For Dummies
  0-7645-5105-1
- Puppies For Dummies
  0-7645-5255-4
- Scrapbooking For Dummies
  0-7645-7208-3
- Senior Dogs For Dummies
  0-7645-5818-8
- Singing For Dummies
  0-7645-2475-5
- 30-Minute Meals For Dummies
  0-7645-2589-1

INTERNET & DIGITAL MEDIA

0-7645-1664-7

0-7645-6924-4

Also available:

- 2005 Online Shopping Directory
  For Dummies
  0-7645-7495-7
- CD & DVD Recording For Dummies
  0-7645-5956-7
- eBay For Dummies
  0-7645-5654-1
- Fighting Spam For Dummies
  0-7645-5965-6
- Genealogy Online For Dummies
  0-7645-5964-8
- Google For Dummies
  0-7645-4420-9

- Home Recording For Musicians
  For Dummies
  0-7645-1634-5
- The Internet For Dummies
  0-7645-4173-0
- iPod & iTunes For Dummies
  0-7645-7772-7
- Preventing Identity Theft For Dummies
  0-7645-7336-5
- Pro Tools All-in-One Desk Reference
  For Dummies
  0-7645-5714-9
- Roxio Easy Media Creator For Dummies
  0-7645-7131-1

SPORTS, FITNESS, PARENTING, RELIGION & SPIRITUALITY

0-7645-5146-9

0-7645-5418-2

Also available:
- Adoption For Dummies
  0-7645-5488-3
- Basketball For Dummies
  0-7645-5248-1
- The Bible For Dummies
  0-7645-5296-1
- Buddhism For Dummies
  0-7645-5359-3
- Catholicism For Dummies
  0-7645-5391-7
- Hockey For Dummies
  0-7645-5228-7

- Judaism For Dummies
  0-7645-5299-6
- Martial Arts For Dummies
  0-7645-5358-5
- Pilates For Dummies
  0-7645-5397-6
- Religion For Dummies
  0-7645-5264-3
- Teaching Kids to Read For Dummies
  0-7645-4043-2
- Weight Training For Dummies
  0-7645-5168-X
- Yoga For Dummies
  0-7645-5117-5

TRAVEL

0-7645-5438-7

0-7645-5453-0

Also available:
- Alaska For Dummies
  0-7645-1761-9
- Arizona For Dummies
  0-7645-6938-4
- Cancún and the Yucatán For Dummies
  0-7645-2437-2
- Cruise Vacations For Dummies
  0-7645-6941-4
- Europe For Dummies
  0-7645-5456-5
- Ireland For Dummies
  0-7645-5455-7

- Las Vegas For Dummies
  0-7645-5448-4
- London For Dummies
  0-7645-4277-X
- New York City For Dummies
  0-7645-6945-7
- Paris For Dummies
  0-7645-5494-8
- RV Vacations For Dummies
  0-7645-5443-3
- Walt Disney World & Orlando For Dummies
  0-7645-6943-0

GRAPHICS, DESIGN & WEB DEVELOPMENT

0-7645-4345-8

0-7645-5589-8

Also available:
- Adobe Acrobat 6 PDF For Dummies
  0-7645-3760-1
- Building a Web Site For Dummies
  0-7645-7144-3
- Dreamweaver MX 2004 For Dummies
  0-7645-4342-3
- FrontPage 2003 For Dummies
  0-7645-3882-9
- HTML 4 For Dummies
  0-7645-1995-6
- Illustrator CS For Dummies
  0-7645-4084-X

- Macromedia Flash MX 2004 For Dummies
  0-7645-4358-X
- Photoshop 7 All-in-One Desk Reference For Dummies
  0-7645-1667-1
- Photoshop CS Timesaving Techniques For Dummies
  0-7645-6782-9
- PHP 5 For Dummies
  0-7645-4166-8
- PowerPoint 2003 For Dummies
  0-7645-3908-6
- QuarkXPress 6 For Dummies
  0-7645-2593-X

NETWORKING, SECURITY, PROGRAMMING & DATABASES

0-7645-6852-3

0-7645-5784-X

Also available:
- A+ Certification For Dummies
  0-7645-4187-0
- Access 2003 All-in-One Desk Reference For Dummies
  0-7645-3988-4
- Beginning Programming For Dummies
  0-7645-4997-9
- C For Dummies
  0-7645-7068-4
- Firewalls For Dummies
  0-7645-4048-3
- Home Networking For Dummies
  0-7645-42796

- Network Security For Dummies
  0-7645-1679-5
- Networking For Dummies
  0-7645-1677-9
- TCP/IP For Dummies
  0-7645-1760-0
- VBA For Dummies
  0-7645-3989-2
- Wireless All In-One Desk Reference For Dummies
  0-7645-7496-5
- Wireless Home Networking For Dummies
  0-7645-3910-8